Dearest M—

A li—

I ho—

come to some peace and
happiness and love for
yourself. You deserve it.

Much love

Yvonne

xxx.

Penguin Books
Listen to Me, Listen to You

Anne Kotzman is senior psychologist at Fairfield House
Rehabilitation Services, where she specializes in the
treatment of work-related stress and injury.

After working as a kindergarten teacher and raising a
family she returned to study, gaining an honours degree
in sociology from Monash University and a B Ed in
counselling from La Trobe University. Later she tutored in
psychology and was student counsellor at the Institute of
Early Childhood Development for twelve years.

Anne Kotzman has run workshops and training seminars
for the Council of Adult Education, Melbourne College of
Advanced Education and a variety of community
groups.

Listen to Me, Listen to You

Anne Kotzman

Penguin Books

Penguin Books Australia Ltd
487 Maroondah Highway, PO Box 257
Ringwood, Victoria, 3134, Australia
Penguin Books Ltd
Harmondsworth, Middlesex, England
Viking Penguin Inc.
40 West 23rd Street, New York, NY 10010, USA
Penguin Books Canada Limited
2801 John Street, Markham, Ontario, Canada, L3R 1B4
Penguin Books (N.Z.) Ltd
182–190 Wairau Road, Auckland 10, New Zealand

First published by Penguin Books Australia, 1989

Copyright © Anne Kotzman, 1989

Typeset in 10½ pt Plantin and 9 pt Avant Garde by
Abb-Typesetting Pty. Ltd, Collingwood, Victoria
Made and printed in Australia by
Australian Print Group, Victoria

CIP

Kotzman, Anne.
Listen to me, listen to you.

Bibliography.
ISBN 0 14 012218 4.

1. Self-respect. 2. Listening. 3. Assertiveness (Psychology).
I. Title.

158.1

Dedication

This book is dedicated to my remarkable parents.

My father was Bill Carrington. People often tell me how they sought his assistance during a particularly difficult time, perhaps facing an illness or death, a crumbling marriage, a broken love affair or a spiritual crisis. Invariably they recall how much he had helped them.

As a child I often saw people arrive to see him, looking downcast and miserable, yet they frequently looked alert and purposeful when they left. I marvelled at this and wondered what he did. Later I realized that he didn't fix people up or rescue them as I had thought, but because he listened with understanding and acceptance, people were able to become more appreciative of themselves, more open to creative ways of dealing with life and more trusting of their own inner wisdom.

My mother, Lorraine Carrington, is less well known. She is an outstanding woman, although she would be the last to acknowledge it.

Women in her day were brought up to be self-effacing and obedient, and to live in the service of others; yet there was an occasion when, as a shy young woman, she resisted the considerable pressure of Victorian society, in particular her father, and refused to 'promise to obey'!

She has always cared deeply for others and enjoyed giving generously of herself in a variety of ways. As a result, her own considerable talents and interests often took second place.

She is in her eighties now and is becoming more assertive about how she feels and what she needs – a change which is welcomed by those who care for her. She is a living example that we need not be stuck with the way we were brought up to be. People can and do continue to change and develop, and they discover new ways of being throughout the whole of life.

Foreword

During the twenty-odd years that I spent in the counselling profession in Australia extraordinarily dramatic and diverse changes in attitudes and practices took place.

In 1961, the pre-requisite for my first job as an assistant student counsellor was membership of the British Psychological Society which, in turn, required an entrance fee and a university degree with a major in psychology. The curious assumption was that, despite an almost total absence of training in the clinical and counselling areas, undergraduate studies in psychology somehow fitted you to operate with expertise in these fields. There was also a somewhat resentful deferral towards the psychiatric profession, leading psychologists to concentrate on their own particular territory of intelligence, vocational and personality testing.

One result of this situation was that I (and many of my peers, as I discovered later) spent many of my early working years in a fairly anxious state, wondering what I should actually be doing and saying to be useful. However, help was on the way, mostly from North America.

Ideas about human relationships and communication were filtering through from a growing number of intelligent, creative and humane thinkers – Carl Rogers, Fritz Perls, Jay Haley, Eric Ericson, Don Jackson spring to mind as early examples – who were less concerned with theoretical explanations of the causes of people's behaviour and were more interested in what went on between people and what made relationships, therapeutic or otherwise, successful or not.

The heady years of the 1960s and 1970s saw wave after wave of new ideas, new evidence and a growing conviction that effective relationships need not be a matter of luck or genes. The psychoanalytic hour on the couch and the psychological test battery receded as models for counsellors and gave way to more human, realistic and effective approaches.

As time went on, a second major generation of workers in the field began to develop models which translated and synthesized these new approaches into practical techniques for counsellors, group leaders, teachers – anyone interested in helping others – become more competent in managing their own lives and relationships. A central theme in all these models was that effective counselling or communication involves a set of clear skills, which may occur naturally in some people to a greater or lesser extent, but which can be identified, understood and learned. Skills such as effective listening, clearing up ambiguities, paraphrasing and summarizing are now familiar and reassuring tools for the craft of counselling as much as for the general business of human beings communicating with and relating to each other.

Teacher and student, parent and child, nurse and patient, coach and athlete, personnel manager and employee – all have the need to understand each other and accurately convey ideas and feelings back and forth.

In other words, the last twenty years have seen the development of a demonstrably successful skills-based approach to counselling and, perhaps better still, the recognition that these basic skills have universal relevance for ordinary people going about their everyday business. Human relations groups, parent effectiveness training, assertiveness courses, lay counselling skills courses and a myriad of other activities reflect this awareness.

All of which brings me, finally, to Anne Kotzman and this book. She has brought together her own version of these things in a way which captures the essence of what makes communication between people work. She has brought a personal warmth and experience to the writing which is reflected in the down-to-earth and strong way with which she leads the reader on a journey of exploration through this complicated territory.

I wonder who you, her readers, will be. I wish that there had been such a book when I started counselling, and I imagine that most professionals have something to learn from it still. It will have great appeal to those in jobs that require 'people skills' and who may have had no formal training for the task. It's also a rewarding read for anyone interested in learning to be better at getting on with others.

Anyway, it's a lovely book written by a warm and wise person who offers a practical set of ideas and approaches that will open some exciting doors for many. Enjoy it!

Jon Frederick

Contents

Contents

Acknowledgements

My thanks to all the people who helped me get this book written and published.

Very special thanks go to: Diane Bretherton and Jon Frederick for the ideas that started the process, Jill Rodd, Liz Norris, Alan Browne and the many other users and readers who have made such enthusiastic and encouraging comments, Lindsay Gore for providing a haven, Simon Kneebone for the graphics, the Institute of Early Childhood Development for providing the time and facilities for writing the original books and for printing and distribution over the years, and to Robert Bolton and Madelyn Burley-Allen for permission to use freely any of their material.

I would also like to acknowledge: A. Combs, D. I. Avila and W. W. Purkey for extracts from *Helping Relationships*, Allyn & Bacon, Boston, Massachusetts, 1975; Erich Fromm for extracts from *Man for Himself*, Fawcett World Library, New York, NY, 1970; Thomas Gordon for 'The Typical Twelve Blocks to Communication' from *P.E.T.: Parent Effectiveness Training*, Peter Wyden, New York, NY, 1970; D. W. Johnson, for extracts from *Reaching Out: Interpersonal Effectiveness and Self-Actualization* (3rd edn), Prentice-Hall, Englewood Cliffs, NY, 1986; Virginia Satir for the poems, 'I am Me' and 'The Five Freedoms' from *Making Contact*, Celestial Arts, California, 1976.

Disclaimer

Every effort has been made to acknowledge the source of material that is not original to this book, however, many of the terms and ideas are so commonly used that the original source is uncertain. The author and publishers would be pleased to hear from copyright holders to rectify any errors or omissions.

Introduction

Many people express, in one way or another, a lack of self-esteem of such a degree that it interferes with optimal functioning in their personal and professional lives.

Low self-esteem can be manifested in a variety of ways from anxiety and over-conscientiousness to conformity, fear of failure and sometimes even illness. When people feel personally inadequate, they often feel resentful and hostile. They may behave in negative, dominant and aggressive ways or they may be self-effacing and withdrawn, or flip from one to the other.

When one's self-esteem is low it is difficult to disentangle from oneself sufficiently to be able to listen clearly and with understanding to other people. One's own feelings are likely to distort the message. The importance of being able to communicate effectively and the repercussions of poor communication skills are well expressed in the following passage from Robert Bolton's excellent book *People Skills*:

Ineffective communication causes an interpersonal gap that is experienced in all facets of life and in all sections of society. Loneliness, family problems, vocational incompetence and dissatisfaction, psychological stress, physical illness, and even death result when communication breaks down. In addition to the personal frustration and the heartache resulting from it, the interpersonal gap is now one of the major social problems of our troubled society.

Communication is the life-blood of every relationship. When open, clear, sensitive communication takes place the relationship is nurtured. When communication is guarded, hostile or ineffective, the relationship falters ...

When communication skills are lacking, there is so much lost love – between spouses, lovers, friends, parents and children. For satisfying relationships, it is essential to discover methods that will help us to at least partially bridge the interpersonal gaps that separate us from others.

Self-esteem begins to develop at a very early age. People who relate closely with young children therefore, whether they be parents, or friends, or teachers, have a very special responsibility. As an adult you *can* change or modify the behaviour you learnt as a child but it is hard work.

This book is about people – about me and you – and about how we can become more understanding and appreciative of ourselves and one another, and how we can learn to tune in and listen in ways which maximize mutual respect and self-esteem, and minimize misunderstandings.

Listen to Me, Listen to You is based on two small books, *Self-Assertion* and *Reflective Listening*, which were initially written to introduce student teachers to the importance of high self-esteem in human development, to the interrelationship between self-esteem and styles of communication, and to some practical listening and assertion skills. Over the years the demand for these books has far exceeded initial expectations.

In its earlier format it has been used extensively in a wide variety of areas ranging from staff training to tertiary education and community based programmes, and of course by individuals wanting to get along better with friends and family. *Listen to Me, Listen to You* is suitable for people from all walks of life who are interested in how they feel about themselves and how to relate to other people with more understanding. It is an easy book for busy people to read because it is clear, simple and comprehensive, and full of practical suggestions. The book is divided into three main parts.

Part I on self-esteem deals with some ideas and information about developing a firm sense of your own instrinsic worth as a person. Suggestions are made about ways of being more comfortable with and appreciative of yourself. Learning to improve your own self-image means that you are more able to develop your own potential as a human being and to use yourself as a facilitator of a positive self-image in others. One's view of oneself is learned and can be modified or changed by relearning. One way of learning to respect and value yourself more is by changing your own behaviour in small but important ways, particularly in ways which improve relationships with other people. In order to do this you may need to increase your social competence by learning better communication skills. Two aspects of communication, listening and self-assertion, are dealt with separately in part II and part III.

Part II on reflective listening is a simple, lucid summary of some of the skills involved in attending and listening, the effects of different ways of responding, and some of the assumptions and attitudes involved. It deals with the way we receive a message and how to respond so that people feel that they have been understood. Good listening says: Tell me about yourself; how you feel; what you need; what you want, think or believe. This section includes some simple activities you can practise to learn these skills.

Part III on self-assertion introduces some of the values and skills of assertiveness training. Assertion is defined as expressing yourself appropriately with respect for the rights of others. It is clearly distinguished from aggression, with which it is often confused.

Self-assertion deals with sending a message about oneself. It says in essence: This is me at this moment. This is how I feel; what I need; what I want, think or believe. This section also includes some practical skills you can practise and learn.

Obviously the separation of assertion and listening is an arbitrary one, made merely for the sake of convenience. In real life, communication involves both listener and speaker expressing, listening, and responding concurrently. These cannot really be separated as they are aspects of a complex interactive process. Keep this in mind as you read the book.

You may not want to use the book in the order in which it is arranged. You could start in the middle or at the end. You may be doing a course which covers one section only or you may feel that one section is of more concern to you than others. Start wherever you like, but be sure you read through the other sections as well to balance out the picture.

The skills described seem very simple, but they need to be practised to integrate them into your personal style. This book is an introduction to the topic. It can be used within a class or group, or you could read it on your own or with a friend.

I hope it will whet your appetite for further reading and practice. At the end is a list of my favourite books and tapes to help you explore topics in greater depth and also a more extensive list of bibliographical sources.

SELF-ESTEEM

YOU CAN LEARN TO FEEL BETTER ABOUT YOURSELF AND BE MORE CONFIDENT

DO YOU THINK EVERYONE ELSE COPES BETTER THAN YOU DO?

DO YOU FEEL UNLOVABLE OR UNLOVED?

DO YOU FIND YOURSELF APOLOGIZING FOR EXISTING?

DO YOU FEEL INFERIOR?

DO YOU THINK YOUR OPINION IS NOT WORTH EXPRESSING?

ARE YOU AFRAID OF MAKING A FOOL OF YOURSELF?

DO YOU BELITTLE YOUR VICTORIES AND EMPHASIZE YOUR FAILURES?

DOES ANXIETY INHIBIT YOUR PERFORMANCE?

DOES GUILT HOLD YOU BACK?

DO YOU FEEL FRIGHTENED OF SPEAKING IN A LARGE GROUP?

DO YOU REALLY VALUE YOURSELF?

Low Self-Esteem: A Common Problem

Most of us at times lack self-confidence, feel highly anxious, have a low sense of self-worth, and find it hard to communicate directly to others about how we feel or what we want.

In our society this applies particularly to women and to people involved in nurturing occupations such as child-care, nursing, teaching, mothering, social work and counselling in which helping and caring for others is the primary focus. In these situations looking after yourself tends to get forgotten or it is seen as selfish and therefore not acceptable.

For some people this sense of personal inadequacy is all-embracing, pervading almost every aspect of their lives. Others feel this way from time to time or in specific kinds of situations, for example, in large groups, in situations involving assessment such as exams or teaching rounds, going for interviews, or perhaps when dealing with 'experts' or people in authority. Probably most of us feel unsure of ourselves and are unable to be assertive at some time or another; and it's not a very pleasant feeling. You may feel childish and stupid, scared of doing the wrong thing and of being rejected. You may get annoyed with yourself and feel you've let yourself down. You may feel that everyone else is much more competent and confident than you are. Feeling different from others can be a lonely position to be in and may increase your isolation and sense of worthlessness. It's easy to get caught in a vicious circle where low self-esteem leads to lack of confidence, anxiety and tension, and poor performance, which in turn increases low self-esteem – and so it continues.

People react in different ways to feelings of inadequacy. You may withdraw and keep your feelings and opinions to yourself, regretting later that you didn't speak up; or perhaps when you feel really overlooked, helpless and frustrated, you burst out and attack someone else, then feel guilty later about being aggressive. Either way, you probably end up feeling just as bad, if not worse, about yourself. Maybe your relationship with another person is damaged as well, which further increases your bad feelings.

As you read this you may be saying to yourself, 'Yes, this is me all over, but so what? There's nothing I can do about it. It's just the way I am'.

This is not entirely true. The way you see yourself is learned and what is learned can be unlearned and relearned. You *can* change if you really want to. If you have learned some things in the past which are not accurate or useful to you in the present, you can learn to be different. It may take time, particularly if your initial learning was very thorough or you are an older person or if the particular learning is very widely generalized to all aspects of your life.

You are stuck with yourself but you can modify parts of yourself which you decide you don't like. You can learn to know and like yourself better, to be aware of your strengths, to appreciate and enjoy your own uniqueness, and to care for yourself. Sometimes only very small changes are all that are needed for important new directions to open up.

You can learn new attitudes and skills which enable you to feel more confident and assured, to communicate more directly and effectively, and to stand up for yourself.

This section of the book deals with some ideas and information about developing a firm sense of your own intrinsic worth as a person. The importance of building up good feelings about yourself is stressed because the way we perceive the world and the way we relate to others is always in terms of how we feel about ourselves.

How Important Is It?

You may ask, 'Why is it so important for me to like myself and have a sense of my own worth? Isn't it more important how I treat other people?' In a book called *Helping Relationships* Combs, Avila and Purkey point out that:

The most important single factor affecting behavior is the self-concept. What people do at every moment of their lives is a product of how they see themselves and the situations they are in ... the self is the star of every performance, the central figure in every act.

Self-concept refers to the organization of all the perceptions and judgements about a person which seem to define for them who they are. It acts like a screen through which everything else is seen, heard, evaluated and understood. We use it as a yardstick for making judgements about the world. Others are seen as taller or shorter, smarter, more or less capable or acceptable, in relation to the way we judge ourselves.

The experience of psychologists, therapists and others who study people supports the notion that mental health, and indeed general health and wellbeing and the ability to live productively and relate to others, derives from the quality of a person's feelings about themselves. Combs, Avila and Purkey put it this way:

It would be hard, indeed, to overestimate the importance of a positive view of self for effective behavior. The self is the center of a person's existence, his frame of reference for dealing with life. Persons who approach their problems with an air of 'can do' are already far ahead of those who begin with a 'can't do' attitude, expecting defeat. With a positive view of self one can dare, be open to experience, and confront the world with open arms and quiet certainty. Negative views of self may lock a person in a vicious circle in which his efforts to deal with life are always too little, too late, or inappropriate.

Virginia Satir, a world-renowned and widely loved American psychologist, with a lifetime of experience as family therapist, peacemaker and writer, spoke often about the central importance of self-esteem. She observed that low self-esteem was a critical component in all troubled families. She believed that all life problems, including wars and suicides, result in part from a low sense of self-worth, particularly when it is covered up and not talked about and so compounded by loneliness and isolation.

> The most important and vital resource
> that you have
> IS
> YOUR SELF.
>
> Care for it!

Your own experience and your own unique response to life is the primary value which you bring to being with others. You may learn various techniques and skills for helping others, but these tend to be meaningless if you can't give of yourself. Combs, Avila and Purkey compare having a high degree of self-esteem with owning a stout ship:

With a sturdy vessel under foot one may go sailing far from shore. When one has doubts about his ship and concern about its seaworthiness, he must play it safe and stay close to harbor. Self-esteem is like that. It is a firm foundation from which to deal with the problems of life with security and sureness.

Some teachers once asked a group of children, 'What can you do about it if you have a bad grade in spelling?' Children with a positive self-image and a history of success suggested all kinds of possibilities, for example, 'Study harder,' 'Ask my teacher,' 'Practise,' 'Ask my mother to help me,' 'Try to find out what I am doing wrong,' and so on. Children who had a negative self-concept and a history of failure replied without exception, 'Nothing!' They had no options to try, no hope, and they gave up immediately, thereby adding further to their experience of failure and inadequacy and validating their view of themselves as powerless and impotent.

Building self-esteem, increasing our understanding of ourselves and others and facilitating appropriate human behaviour are becoming increasingly vital responsibilities for us all.

Acquiring Self-Esteem

A person's temperament is probably largely inherited. Temperament may influence the way we view the world including our view of ourselves, nevertheless the actual thoughts and beliefs we have about ourselves which contribute to our sense of self-esteem are largely learned. This is fortunate because they can be relearned.

Self-esteem is learned from the accumulation of experiences one has of self in relation to mastering one's world. It starts at a very early age from the close and significant people on whom a small child is dependent for survival; first of all parents, and later brothers and sisters, teachers, friends, and so on. A low sense of self-esteem is usually acquired from significant others who feel inferior about themselves and who, as a result, are defensive and destructive in their relationships, putting other people down, or insisting on unrealistic perfectionist standards of achievement.

A low self-image does not mean that you are no good, but rather that your learning situation was a negative one. Often parents and teachers are simply unaware of the destructive and debilitating effects of continual criticism and failure. They may have the false belief that failure is good for people, that it builds character and courage and is a valuable stimulant for growth. Similarly, they may believe that children will get 'swelled heads' or 'too big for their boots' or 'cocky' if their successful efforts are praised and they experience the joy of success. These beliefs are false.

Cocksure people are so uncertain of themselves that they continually try to convince themselves and others of their superior qualities. Low self-esteem is learned by repeated experience of failure leading to further lack of confidence, feelings of inadequacy and further failure – a downward spiral.

A Spiral Model of Personal Development

What we have been talking about can be seen as a vicious circle of development. Personal development is a matter of the interaction of different aspects of the self and the environment. A circular or spiral model is a useful way of making sense of what happens.

This sort of simple model can be applied in many different ways. For example, we can look at the self as, in part, an outcome of the interplay or interaction of thoughts, feelings and actions, or behaviour.

The advantage of this model is that it allows us to see the self as a system. It shows how intervention and change at any point in the system will have repercussions in other parts of the system. Changes in thinking bring about changes in behaviour and feelings. If behaviour is changed, thoughts and feelings change too, and so on.

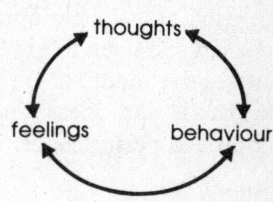

This is a more useful way of looking at personal development than the conventional linear model based on cause and effect. The linear model may overemphasize the role of past experience in determining personality and fail to account for the degree of change which people can initiate throughout the life span.

A developmental spiral can move in an upward, positive direction or in a downward, negative direction. This is what is meant by benign and vicious circles.

Let's look at the vicious circle of low self-esteem and inadequacy, and how it perpetuates itself. In a circular model you can start or finish anywhere; it is the process and direction which is important. Let us say you have a low opinion of yourself, this leads to lack of confidence in your own powers or ability to cope, this leads to feelings of hopelessness and expectations of failure, these lead to anxiety and tension, which freeze you up. Freezing up blocks the free use of your knowledge and creativity, and your freedom to improvise or experiment with a variety of options.

The outcome is poor performance which reinforces your already low sense of personal worth. Any criticism appears as further evidence of your incompetence and you are unable to use it constructively. A difficult situation is perceived as a threat rather than a challenge, and all your energy is expended in defending yourself and coping with fear. Instead of learning from your mistakes and gaining competence, you learn that you are

13

even more inadequate and worthless than you thought. And so it goes on – this is the vicious circle. Does it sound familiar?

A benign circle, on the other hand, moves in the opposite direction towards increased competence, confidence and self-esteem. A difficult situation is seen as a challenge. Mistakes can be used as valuable opportunities for learning. The person is relaxed and open to experience, feeling free to play around with alternative modes of coping. Energy is directed towards the task in hand, and ideas and knowledge flow freely, leading to improved performance, which further enhances self-esteem.

When you are caught in a vicious circle, the important thing to know is that you can change. The downward spiral can be reversed so that you *feel* better about yourself, you *think* more creatively and more rationally and *behave* more appropriately and constructively – in other words, a downward spiral can be reversed into an upward spiral.

Can I Really Change?

When you get caught in vicious circles like this you can change the direction of your development if you decide to. You don't have to be stuck with low self-esteem.

You probably learned to be the way you are because of the people around you and the kinds of experiences you had. When you were a child you were helpless and dependent and couldn't do much to alter the situation you were in. But you are no longer a child.

Now that you are an adult you have the power to reverse the pattern of events. You can see that your view of yourself is not an accurate or objective evaluation of the way you really are, but rather an indicator of the kind of experiences you've had and the way you've learned to view yourself. You cannot undo the past, but you can exert some control on the present and your directions in the future.

There is no best way to change. The thought–feeling–behaviour cycle can be interrupted at any point. Different approaches suit different people and different situations. If you change the way you *think* about yourself, your feelings and behaviour will change. If you change the way you *behave*, you will feel and think differently about yourself, and so on. You can try a variety of ways to find out what works best for you.

In this part of the book the main emphasis is on changing the way you *think* and *feel* about yourself. Parts II and III look at how you can change the way you *behave* in relation to others. It may sound easy, but most people find it very difficult to change. This is not surprising because we are trying to change long-established habits and attitudes, probably learned in childhood and reinforced ever since. Changing means leaving behind the familiar and taking a leap of faith into the unknown with no guarantees. Fear of change is evident in a range of well-known proverbs, for example, 'Better the devil you know than the one you don't'. Even if the known and the familiar is not entirely satisfactory, at least it seems safe. Then there is always the question, 'How do I know people will still like me if I change?' You don't know, and they may not. The only way you will find out is to try. If it is good for you, those who really love and respect you will value your efforts to tap your real potential. Putting their genuine caring to the test can be pretty scary in itself, but if their goodwill is dependent on you feeling and acting inferior and being only half what you could be, then you have to make a decision about whether it is worth having. There are plenty of people in the world who will like the new you, particularly if you become happier and more at peace with yourself.

Knowing that change can be difficult will help you to be persistent and to cope with the feelings that crop up. Don't expect to change too much or too quickly. Personal progress is seldom smooth. Two steps forward and one step back is a common experience. It is the direction of change and the small steps taken which are significant, not the amount of change.

How Do I Start?

If you have decided that you are in a vicious circle of low self-esteem, the first step towards tapping your full potential is your decision that you want to change. This means being prepared to take action and try out different things and to take responsibility for yourself.

The main attitude required is openness – being open to new possibilities and new attitudes, trying them out, adjusting them to fit, practising them and using them. Openness to experience involves dropping 'shoulds' and 'oughts' from your vocabulary and moving into becoming more aware of what you feel and what you want. It means moving away from blaming the way you are on others or the past and moving towards accepting responsibility for yourself and focusing on the present – how things really are and how you would like them to be different. It means trusting and valuing your own experience, feeling what you feel, and deciding how you will act.

The first step could be to be open with yourself and to take a good clear look at yourself.

This does not mean making a list of your faults and weaknesses. On the contrary, this is the biased view of yourself that you're trying to correct. It means approaching yourself in a respectful, tolerant and accepting way, looking particularly at your strengths, in order to redress the balance. People with low self-esteem often find it very difficult to find things they like about themselves because they are so used to defining themselves in terms of their inadequacies. So this is an important exercise.

> ## Self-acceptance is a key.

Paradoxically, acceptance is a prerequisite for change. When you can really accept yourself as you are, then you can start to change some aspects that you see as holding you back. If you are totally self-rejecting you're not open enough, or hopeful enough, to be able to change. Most of your energy will be going into hating yourself or propping up your shaky self-esteem.

So now could be the time to be a little kinder to yourself. You might like to ask yourself, 'What is the smallest change I could make which would make a difference to the way I feel about myself?' Then you might like to experiment with this small change and see what happens.

Will I Become Too Selfish?

When people hear that it is important to like and respect themselves and to become aware of their own feelings and needs, they often worry about being selfish. Most of us have been brought up to believe that it is 'bad' to be selfish and 'good' to deny ourselves. People say, 'Isn't it bad to love yourself? Shouldn't you love others and stop thinking about yourself?' We have all heard parental, religious or other authoritarian voices saying these things.

There is a great deal of confusion about the nature of selfishness and selflessness. Self-love is not the same as selfishness. The notion that it is, is based on the assumption that love is a finite commodity that comes in fixed amounts; there is only so much to go round and if some of that is spent on oneself, others will be deprived.

> ## Love is not finite.

Love is an infinite, creative, self-generating force, and the paradox of love is that it is catchy and transforms all it touches. The more it is experienced and expressed the more there is.

Erich Fromm, in his book *Man For Himself*, explains how caring for oneself and respecting one's own uniqueness cannot be separated from caring for and respecting another individual. He points out that the notion that love for oneself and love for others are mutually exclusive is a logical fallacy. If it is a virtue to love others as humans, it must equally be a virtue to love one's self as human. He firmly believed that genuinely loving people love and respect themselves as well as others. Even in the Bible it says love one another as thyself, not instead of.

Genuine love implies care, respect, responsibility and knowledge. It is an actual striving for the growth and happiness of the loved person and is rooted in one's own capacity. Fromm believed that the essence of the capacity to love is the ability to affirm one's own life and respect one's own freedom and growth, to the extent that if a person loves only others, that person cannot really love at all.

Selfishness is really the opposite of self-love. Selfish people love themselves too little; in fact, they hate, neglect and deny themselves, as do unselfish or selfless people. This leaves them empty and frustrated, trying to snatch from life small satisfactions to fill the emptiness.

In my own experience I know that when I feel good about myself, or when I am 'in love' – that is when I am being with another in a mutual state of loving – I love the whole world. I feel rich, expansive, productive, caring and overflowing. When my self-image is low, I feel inadequate, restricted, mean and tight, and then I am much more likely to be uncaring of others because I am concentrating on wanting to fill my own emptiness. Selfishness and selflessness are both exploitive. Selfish people exploit others and diminish themselves. Selfless people exploit themselves and diminish others.

This may seem surprising. Fromm mentions the effect of unselfish or selfless mothers on their children:

The children [of the 'unselfish' mother] do not show the happiness of persons who are convinced that they are loved; they are anxious, tense, afraid of mother's disapproval, and anxious to live up to her expectations. Usually, they are affected by their mother's hidden hostility against life. Worse, the mother's unselfishness prevents the children from criticizing her. They are put under an obligation not to disappoint her; they are taught, under the mask of virtue, dislike for life. If one has a chance to study the effect of a mother with genuine self-love, one can see that there is nothing more conducive to giving a child the experience of what love, joy and happiness are, than being loved by a mother who loves herself.

It is easy to see how this applies not only to the relationship between mothers and children but also within all sorts of relationships.

Developing Self-Esteem

So you have decided you want to improve your self-esteem. You are ready for action, and you're wondering what to do.

Before you start learning and practising the new communication and behavioural skills outlined in parts II and III you might like to start changing the way you think and feel about yourself by doing some of the following exercises.

The Five Freedoms To start the process of enhancing self-esteem you might like to give yourself a present. Here are Five Freedoms, which are everyone's right. They are from Virginia Satir's book, *Making Contact*.

The freedom to see and hear what is here
   instead of what should be, was, or will
   be.

The freedom to say what one feels and
thinks
   instead of what one should.

The freedom to feel what one feels
   instead of what one ought.

The freedom to ask for what one wants
   instead of always waiting for permission.

The freedom to take risks in one's own
behalf
   instead of choosing to be only 'secure'
   and not rocking the boat.

You are Unique Remind yourself that your value lies in your
uniqueness and that you have value just by being yourself, quite

apart from anything you might or might not achieve. The following poem from *Making Contact* celebrates this theme.

I AM ME

In all the world, there is no one else exactly like me.
There are persons who have some parts like me,
but no one adds up exactly like me.
Therefore, everything that comes out of me is
authentically mine because I alone chose it.
I own everything about me –
my body, including everything it does;
my mind, including all its thoughts and ideas;
my eyes, including the images of all they behold;
my feelings, whatever they may be –
anger, joy, frustration, love, disappointment, excitement;
my mouth, and all the words that come out of it,
polite, sweet, or rough, correct or incorrect;
my voice, loud or soft;
and all my actions, whether they be to others or to myself.

I own my fantasies, my dreams, my hopes, my fears,
I own all my triumphs and successes,
all my failures and mistakes.
Because I own all of me
I can become intimately acquainted with me.
By so doing I can love me
and be friendly with me in all my parts.

I can then make it possible for all of me
to work in my best interests.
I know there are aspects about myself that puzzle me,
and other aspects I do not know.
But as long as I am friendly and loving to myself
I can courageously and
hopefully look for the solutions to the puzzles
and for ways to find out more about me.

However I look and sound, whatever I say or do,
and whatever I think and feel
at a given moment in time is me.
This is authentic and represents where I am
at that moment in time.
When I review later how I looked and sounded,
what I said and did, and how I thought and felt
some parts may turn out to be unfitting.

I can discard that which is unfitting
and keep that which proved fitting,
and invent something new for that which I discarded.
I can see, hear, feel, think, say, and do.
I have the tools to survive, to be close to others,
to be productive, and to make sense and order
out of the world of people and things outside of me.
I own me,
and therefore I can engineer me.
I am me
and I am okay.

Virginia Satir

Set a New Goal Make the preservation and enhancement of self-esteem a goal for yourself and others around you. Talk straight to people. Use your new awareness of the importance of feeling good about yourself to communicate to others. Tell them what you feel, things you like about them, and so on.

This is not to suggest that you distribute empty flattery, which, being phoney, makes no one feel good; but rather that you give others genuine positive feedback. It is important too for your own self-esteem to learn to accept compliments graciously, without giggling or denial.

Know Yourself Spend some time getting to know yourself as you really are. Think about the kind of things you like doing. Think of some of the times when you felt relaxed and happy – not when you think you ought to have been happy, but when you really were. It might have been something very simple that gave you pleasure. It might have involved solitude or having lunch with a friend or doing nothing at all.

Personal Strengths Make a list or talk with an understanding friend about your own personal strengths, that is, aspects of yourself that you like and enjoy. You may find this difficult if your view of yourself is very negative, but don't give up. Even the act of trying to focus on your strengths will be useful. You may need to think of the positive aspects of qualities which you rate as negative, for example, shyness may be a negative in some situations but it also involves sensitivity which can be a very positive quality. It is important that you stop putting yourself down and start being more appreciative of yourself. It may help if you identify the aspects of yourself that you really want to preserve.

Relaxation Learn to relax. It helps you to get in touch with your inner self and become more at ease. It is also useful to learn to remain cool and calm in stressful situations.

You can learn relaxation by joining a relaxation class, learning yoga or meditation, listening to relaxation tapes or records or reading books on relaxation and stress management.

Once you've experienced deep relaxation you can learn with practice to recall this feeling at will.

Another relaxation technique is to imagine a calm scene. Relax yourself, then imagine in as much detail and vividness as you can, using all your senses, some situation in which you were really relaxed and at ease. You might recall lying in a warm bath or lying in the sun on a beach or relaxing in front of a fire with some nice people. It should be a quiet place, in which you feel very good, very alive, calm and self-confident. If you can't recall a real scene like this, create one in your imagination. Practise it often.

When you find yourself in a situation in which you feel nervous or uptight, take a few deep breaths and bring this scene back into your awareness. As you create this picture in all its detail, let the associated feelings of peace and tranquillity flow through you.

Self-Talk Observe how you talk to yourself, silently in your head. We all have sentences going through our heads most of the time.

Albert Ellis, the father of rational emotive therapy, calls this process 'self-talk'. He claims that most people 'catastrophize' and predict to themselves all kinds of calamities. He believes that there are very few real disasters in life and that much of our self-talk is irrational and exaggerated. He believes that by changing our self-talk to more realistic predictions we are more likely to maintain our self-esteem and manage the situation better.

Listen to your thoughts when anticipating a situation that you fear and practise adjusting your self-talk. For example: You have to make a speech or go for a job interview. Your thoughts may be something like this, 'I'll never manage to remember what I want to say, I'll be nervous and confused, I'll go red in the face. Everyone will think I'm stupid and that will be a disaster. I really am totally hopeless and I'll never be any good'.

If you find this sort of monologue going through your head, you can re-programme your thoughts to something more realistic, such as, 'I might forget *some* of it. I might be nervous to begin with but I do know some ways to relax myself. I may get a bit confused and that could be a pity, but I'll be able to handle most of it reasonably well. I may go red in the face, but this is no disaster. I may not impress some people, but this doesn't mean I am a stupid person. I would like to handle this situation well and achieve my goals. If I don't I will be disappointed, but it won't be the end of the world'.

Sometimes it helps to face the worst that could happen. You will usually realize both that it is unlikely and that it would not really be a total disaster, merely unpleasant.

Identify Problem Areas Look at factors in your present life situation which might be reinforcing your low self-esteem. Consider what changes could reasonably be made, whether you can change the situation itself or whether you need to change the way you respond to it.

Perhaps you would find it useful to discuss your feelings with the people involved. Part III of this book outlines some techniques to help you do this. The Five-Star Plan for approaching situations assertively is particularly useful in planning what you want to say and how to say it.

Take Off Your Dark Glasses If you have the habit of focusing on your mistakes and ignoring or trivializing your contribution to success, interrupt this and try a more realistic and balanced formula for self-assessment. At the end of a day or on the completion of a task, ask yourself:

What did I like about what I did?

What would I like to do differently if the situation was repeated?

What help/information/practice might I need to enable me to do that?

You can also use this formula to assist other people, such as your supervisor, boss or workmates, to assess your work constructively. Ask questions such as, 'What did you like about how I ...' or 'What would you like me to do differently?'

Spot the Danger Signals Watch for flashing red lights. Become aware of when and how you put yourself down. Do you often say:

I'm sorry but ...

I'm probably wrong as usual, but ...

You may not believe this, but ...

This may sound silly, but ...

I wouldn't know anything about it really, but ...

These, and similar statements, are qualifiers and by using them you undermine yourself and what you are saying. They communicate that you consider you are not worth taking seriously.

Knowing yourself is important if you want to change. Keep a record of when and with whom you tend to speak like this. If you are very brave you could tape-record a conversation and listen to the way you communicate – your speech patterns, hesitations, intonation and so on. Then you could play around with trying out new, more confident sounding ways of saying what you mean, without undermining yourself. Sometimes work-oriented people forget the value of play. Playing is not only enjoyable and relaxing, it's a great way to learn as well.

Be Realistic Don't tackle too much at once. Practise small steps at a time. Don't worry if you slide back. Making mistakes is part of learning. Each time you fall back into old habits you can become aware more quickly of what has happened and you gradually learn to catch yourself before you fall. Remember, all you are aiming for at this stage is to know yourself better and to like yourself more.

Ask for Help If you feel your problem is severe and you feel totally low and hopeless about helping yourself or if it seems impossible to elicit understanding or positive help from the significant people in your life, then seek appropriate professional assistance to help you explore your difficulties and to support you while you change.

This might be your first and most difficult step in taking care of yourself.

Improve Your Communication Skills Seek to make more satisfactory relationships on all levels, from the everyday interactions with customers, tradespeople, clients and shopkeepers, to friends, family, partners and lovers, by improving communications.

Learn to respect and accept other people, to listen to them non-judgementally, and to respond in ways which enhance mutual understanding and high self-esteem; and which help to bridge the interpersonal gaps that separate people, leaving them feeling lost and lonely.

One of the most effective ways to improve your self-esteem is to learn to be more assertive and to stand up for yourself. Take responsibility for your own feelings by making 'I' statements: 'I feel very inferior when . . . and it is a problem for me' instead of 'You make me feel inferior'. The latter blames the other person and usually draws a defensive or aggressive or argumentative response rather than understanding. Assertiveness is one of the most effective ways to improve your self-esteem.

Parts II and III of this book explore all of the above skills in more detail. Start with whichever part seems most important for you right now. The separation of listening skills and self-assertion skills is an arbitrary separation to enable each to be studied in some detail. In everyday life, of course, both occur simul-taneously and inseparably. They are simply different aspects of the same process.

Most people find reflective listening skills require quite a lot of practice. It is much easier to learn to express oneself, than it is to learn to put one's own judgements on hold and really hear someone else. But don't give up. Once you have mastered part II of this book, you will probably romp through the final section on self-assertion.

You Are Taller Than You Think If you were to allow yourself to agree with this, what differences would it make to the way you feel about yourself and your future directions?

REFLECTIVE LISTENING

HOW CAN I KNOW HOW ANOTHER PERSON FEELS?

WHAT IF I DON'T WANT TO GET INVOLVED OR IF I REALLY HAVEN'T TIME TO LISTEN AT THE MOMENT?

WILL SOMEBODY PLEASE LISTEN TO ME?

WHAT DO YOU SAY TO SOMEONE WHO TELLS YOU HER CHILD HAS DIED?

HOW CAN I HELP SOMEONE SOLVE PERSONAL PROBLEMS?

I OFTEN PRICK PEOPLE'S BUBBLES WHEN THEY SHARE THEIR JOY WITH ME.

I TRY TO DRAW PEOPLE OUT BUT THEY DON'T SEEM TO CONFIDE IN ME.

WHEN PEOPLE GET ANGRY WITH ME I GET VERY DEFENSIVE.

WE ALWAYS SEEM TO GET OUR LINES CROSSED.

WHAT'S WRONG WITH GIVING ADVICE?

WHY AM I SO DISTANT FROM MY CHILDREN?

HOW DO YOU DEAL WITH SILENCE? IT MAKES ME UNCOMFORTABLE.

Introduction

This section focuses on some of the skills required on the receiving or listening side of communication. It looks particularly at how different ways of responding to the messages we receive affect the way we feel about ourselves and others. You will also find out more about the skills involved in one type of listening, reflective or empathic listening:

- What it is,
- Why it is important,
- How to do it,
- When to use it,
- When not to use it.

Listening and self-assertion are two complementary aspects of communication. Obviously it is inaccurate and arbitrary to separate the two processes: a response is in itself a message. Communication is a continuous, simultaneous and complex process.

Communication can go wrong in many different ways, to the extent that it is rather amazing that we ever understand one another at all. We can only know another's inner world of experience indirectly by inference, that is, by decoding or interpreting the meaning of that person's behaviour. Despite the best intentions, misinterpretations and misunderstandings can occur in either the sending or the receiving of information.

Sometimes we are better at one side of the process than the other. A person may be assertive but fail to listen to how others are feeling or conversely, may be an excellent listener but be unable or unwilling to let others know clearly how he or she is feeling.

Goodwill alone is not enough.

To achieve a high level of accuracy in interpreting a person's inner world of meaning, certain skills are needed, particularly

ways of picking up and correcting errors when they occur. These skills can be learned. They seem simple. They *are* simple, but are not always easy to do, particularly when it means unlearning bad habits.

Good listening is more difficult and demanding than it appears to be. It is hard to control the natural tendency to express oneself long enough to concentrate on other people's experience.

When other people express negative feelings or are upset, we tend to search immediately for solutions to the problem, or we try to deny or reduce the intensity of the feelings expressed. When people express great joy we may try to 'bring them down to earth'. It takes respect for other people and a belief in each person's individuality, separateness and personal worth to refrain from trying to blame or rescue and to allow people just to be, to have time and space to work out their own solutions, or even to choose the option of no action at all.

Learning to attend fully to another person, trying to understand and reflect on how the world appears to them, without making judgements or finding solutions for change, requires considerable effort and practice.

Learning to Listen

Is it really necessary to learn to listen? I used to think that good listening was simply a matter of having good hearing and concentration. There were times, however, when I felt that I understood how another person felt but didn't know how to respond or what to say to convey my understanding. I was unaware of some of the different ways of responding and of the impact these could have on the other person, on their sense of self-worth and on the quality of the relationship between us.

People often mistakenly believe that in order to say anything helpful they have to:
- know all the answers,
- come up with solutions,
- make the other person feel better,
- tell them what to do,

and furthermore be right.

How impossible! In reality each person has inner resources for dealing with life situations and it is not usually helpful or appropriate to tell other people what to do or try to fix them up.

In a book called *The Helping Relationship*, Brammer explains that, 'Helping another human being is basically a process of enabling that person to grow in the directions that person chooses, to solve problems, and to face crises'. It has been found that this process occurs most readily when a relationship is established in which the other person feels genuinely understood and accepted.

Perhaps no one can ever fully understand another's world, yet as Gerard Egan puts it, 'there is in all of us a craving to be understood at least by a few people . . . Letting people know that I understand what they are saying to me is a kind of oil that lubricates the entire communication process'.

What is Reflective Listening?

Reflective listening is a particular way of responding to the thoughts and feelings communicated to us by another person, a technique which increases and communicates understanding. It derives originally from the non-directive or client-centred approach to psychotherapy developed and practised by Carl Rogers. He did not use the term reflective listening but referred to responding with understanding or empathy: feeling *with* another person.

Rogers found that when he listened to his clients in a way that communicated genuineness, acceptance and understanding, they were able to experience themselves more fully, to become more aware and accept their feelings better, to clarify confusions and conflicts, and eventually to develop viable solutions to their own problems.

Rogers' quotation from the Chinese philosopher Lao-Tzu expresses the beliefs that emerged from his work with people:

> *If I keep from meddling with people,*
> *they take care of themselves.*

If I keep from commanding people,
  they behave themselves.
If I keep from preaching at people,
  they improve themselves.
If I keep from imposing on people,
  they become themselves.

Reflective listening is known by a number of different names. It is referred to as active listening by Thomas Gordon, founder of the effectiveness programmes; as empathic listening by Rogers, Carkhuff and others; as paraphrasing by Egan; or more simply as listening with understanding. I have chosen to use the term reflective listening, because it has two connotations, both relevant. The act of reflective listening involves the listener in reflecting back, as from a mirror, the speaker's meaning; secondly, this approach to listening requires the listener to enter a reflective, contemplative mode of accepting and 'letting be'.

Learning to be an understanding listener involves more than simply reading about it. It involves:

● attitudes,
● intentions,
● responding skills

You will need to practise and practise often. You will learn the skills more thoroughly if you can practise with a friend or in a small group, as well as practising in everyday life. Some of the exercises will suggest ways of doing this. Feedback, that is, information to you about the other person's response to your response, is an important part of learning.

Don't be put off if at first reflective listening sounds corny and artificial. Like any new skill it needs to be integrated into your own natural style. If it continues to sound artificial then something is wrong. As you are learning, you will need feedback from others to tell you how it sounds to them and how they feel. Do they feel genuinely understood or do they think you are practising some newfangled trick on them? Persevere! Reflective listening well done will not be obvious. As a genuine attempt to create understanding, it can and really does work. Try it and see for yourself.

The attitude and skills described in this part of the book enable people to understand one another better in such ordinary everyday relationships as:

doctor : patient

client : lawyer

customer : shop assistant

builder : tradesperson

student : teacher

worker : boss

friend : friend

parent : child

wife : husband

as well as in situations which involve helping others in distress.

The aim is not to turn readers into psychologists or counsellors but to assist ordinary people to listen and respond accurately to one another, with clarity, warmth and humanity. As Brammer says, 'Helping others is a function of all concerned human beings and is not and, I believe should not be, limited to professionally trained therapists.'

Communication

Before becoming more involved with the topic of reflective listening, let us look very briefly at communication as a whole and at where listening skills fit in.

We cannot *not* communicate. Whenever people see or hear one another they are communicating. The question is not whether to, but how to – how to communicate so that we improve our understanding of others and convey this to them so that they feel understood, misunderstandings are minimized, and each person's self-esteem remains intact. If I am to understand you I will need to try to stand in your shoes as if they were mine and, through interpreting your messages, try to image your experience and what it means to you. Accurate listening is an essential part of the process of attempting to understand another's separate experience, to cross personal boundaries not eliminate them.

Effective communication is not just a matter of luck or something we are born with. We are born with the sensory equipment and the brain structures which enable us to send and receive messages and to code and decode them, but how we do this is a learned skill.

> Most people do not communicate well.

If you do not communicate as well as you would like to, all is not lost; you can change. If some of the ways you have learned to communicate in the past prove to be ineffective or destructive you can unlearn them and relearn new ways. It takes time and effort and the willingness to persevere. You don't have to become an instant expert, but people are often surprised and excited when they get the hang of some of these skills and find that they really work.

Misunderstandings occur in many ways. Sometimes people, particularly young children, are extremely egocentric, so that they see things from one perspective only – their own. They assume that another person's experience is the same as their own, or they attribute their own meanings to the other's action and words. They can be wrong. Errors tend to compound themselves if not picked up and corrected quickly. We are all familiar with the political argument between friends, when neither person is really listening to the other, each one assuming that their words mean the same to the other person. This is intensified when the situation is highly charged emotionally. Certain words may have very different emotional connotations for each person. The people concerned may argue loud and long along two parallel lines which never seem to meet because neither is really understanding the other's meaning or talking about the same thing.

Communication involves two processes, or perhaps two aspects of a process:

- sending,
- receiving.

We are sending messages continually by the way we dress, how we move, our gestures, words, tone of voice, facial expression, etc. – messages telling others about ourselves. Similarly, we are constantly receiving and interpreting the messages sent by others.

One person decides to communicate with another. He or she does so because of an inner state or need. Something is going on inside. The actual state inside that person cannot be communicated directly because it is internal, so the person has to select and send a signal in a code that represents this need or state.

A communication is effective when the receiver interprets a message in the way that the sender intended. At such times, we say that the sender has been understood. This does not always happen, however. Sometimes the receiver imputes a different meaning to the message, that is, decodes it or interprets it inaccurately. When this happens the sender of the message has been misunderstood and communication has broken down, as in the following example:

Mary is hungry. She selects a signal, in this case words, to represent her need. This is called encoding. Suppose Mary says, 'When will dinner be ready?' When Sue receives the coded message she attributes meaning to it in order to try to understand what is going on inside Mary. This is called decoding. If Sue decodes the message accurately she will understand that Mary is hungry and wants to know when she will eat. But she may decode the message incorrectly, that is, attribute a meaning to it that Mary did not intend. She may interpret the message to mean that Mary is criticizing her for not having the meal ready earlier, and she may respond angrily or defensively. In this case the communication has misfired and misunderstanding has occurred. Had the message been encoded or decoded differently Sue may have understood Mary and acknowledged her state. She may have met her need, or at least given her some useful information about her immediate environment – what to expect and how to get her needs met.

Often when inaccuracies in coding occur neither person is aware that a misunderstanding exists, or neither is aware at what point it has occurred. One way to improve this situation is for the receiver of the message to check on the accuracy of the decoding. Sue could have said, 'You're hungry?' and Mary could have confirmed this. Here the two are understanding one another. The message has been received correctly and this has been verified. Mary is likely to feel understood by Sue and may even have a meal ready soon. Sue knows something about what is going on inside Mary and can decide how she will respond, whether she will meet that need or not.

Supposing Sue had similarly checked out her incorrect decoding of Mary's message, she might have said, 'You mean I should have had dinner ready earlier?' Then Mary could have picked up the inaccuracy and corrected it by sending a clearer message with more chance of her inner state being understood and her need being met.

Reflective listening enables a person to pick up errors and correct them before they become magnified.

The receiver *recodes* the received message in their own words and reflects it back to the sender in order to check on whether or not the interpretation has been made correctly. The receiver refrains at this point from sending their own message, whether it be a judgement, an opinion, advice, an analysis, or a statement. Nothing more or less is reflected back than the receiver's interpretation of the sender's message. This does not mean that the receiver responds only to the verbal part of the message. The receiver arrives at the meaning of a message from many cues, including facial expression, tone of voice, posture, gestures, as well as words.

Styles of Response

Most people wonder from time to time about how to help other people, how best to respond when other people are talking about serious personal issues or problems or sharing important feelings.

There are a number of different ways a person might respond when trying to be helpful. How do you normally respond to other people? Do you have one particular style of response that you use in most situations? Do you know what it is? Do you know how other people feel about your responses? Do they see you as understanding or do they commonly describe you in some other way? There may be considerable variations in your style of response depending on the situation and the personalities involved. Don't be concerned if you don't know what is meant by styles of responding; this will become clear as you go along.

Complete the following exercise, which looks at various response styles, before continuing with the rest of the book. It may be interesting to redo the exercise once you have completed part II to see if your response style has changed.

The following exercise contains a set of fifteen brief statements, snippets of conversation about real life situations. Obviously you are required to respond under somewhat artificial constraints. This however has the advantage of helping you learn to respond to the immediate message, rather than feeling obliged or compelled to keep probing for more and more information before you can respond. Of course, in real life you would have access to more information from body language, tone of voice and so on. You may want to alter the situations slightly to fit your own experience.

Your Response Style

Following each statement are five possible responses. Read each statement and the five responses. Select the one response which seems to you the most appropriate reply. Put a ring around the letter of the response you consider best. Instructions for scoring are at the end of the exercise.

1 Margaret

I can't stop Ronnie painting on the walls. He has painting books, he has crayons, pencils, everything.

a How old was he when he started painting on the walls?

b At his age he shouldn't still be painting on the walls. You really shouldn't let him get away with it.

c It's really not fair to you when you've given him so many materials to play with.

41

d Maybe he's acting in a babyish way because he's jealous of the new baby.

e You feel helpless and desperate that in spite of all the things you give him to do he still paints on the walls.

2 John

I sometimes wish I didn't have quite so many jobs coming my way. It's great to be in demand, but there are times when I would like to take it easy.

a You're just feeling that way because of all the articles you've read about people having heart attacks.

b I'm sure you can manage. You've always been able to keep up with things.

c When so many people are unable to get work, you should be thankful that you've got plenty of jobs on hand.

d You've got mixed feelings about having so much work.

e How many new jobs have you had in the last month?

3 Sam

A weekend coming up and I guess Joanna will start her usual – telling my new girl friend to go away.

a It's time she was learning to be a bit more polite to visitors. She needs to be taught how to behave.

b You're worried that Joanna is going to be rude to your friend once again.

c Do you think perhaps she just wants her family all to herself?

d Why do you think she doesn't want visitors around?

e Never mind. I'm sure your new girl friend will understand.

4 Kate

Kids! They look so happy here, but by tea-time they drive me mad.

a Don't let them get you down. They're really good kids.

b Do you spend plenty of time with them in the afternoon?

c Sometimes they just drive you crazy.

d You shouldn't let them get under your skin; it only makes them worse.

e Maybe they get irritable because they have their dinner too late and they're overtired.

5 Stephen

I'm a nervous wreck this week. My wife's mother is coming to stay for three months and Jim and Peter are continually at each other's throats. I just know they'll be at their worst. What am I going to do to preserve my sanity?

a You're dreading the next few months and feeling frazzled already.

b It's good for children to have their grandparents around.

c How long is it since your mother-in-law came to stay?

d I'm sure it will work out just fine and you'll enjoy having Gran to stay. It will be good for the boys too.

e You should have a talk to the boys before their grandmother comes and make sure they're on their best behaviour.

6 Peter

I have the queerest feeling. Whenever anything good happens to me I just can't believe it. I act as though it never happened. And it worries me. I wanted to take Sarah out for dinner. When she said yes I was so flustered that I messed up the whole evening.

a It just doesn't seem real when something good happens.

b You probably feel you don't deserve to have anything good happen and it makes you feel guilty.

c Well, you shouldn't worry about it.

d You've got to grow up and be a bit more realistic about women. She was probably dying to go out with you.

e Are these feelings associated with something that happened in the past? When did they start?

7 Phillip

If we have another early morning scene over what to wear I'll belt those children . . . So help me!

a How many times have they made a scene?

b You get really wild and you're scared you'll do your block one of these days.

c But it's great that they are so keen to dress nicely. You should be pleased.

d Oh! Go on! You know you love those children and they'll grow out of it.

e You get upset because you were never allowed to choose your clothes.

8 Maria

I'm so excited! My sister is coming back to Australia for Christmas and the whole family will be together for a great celebration on Christmas Day.

a You poor girl; you must have been very lonely here without all your relatives.

b Is Christmas an important custom in your culture?

c It's just great to have her come back at this time and have the whole family all together at last.

d You want to have all your relatives together so you feel that you belong here.

e It's not good to get too excited about things. You get too easily disappointed.

9 Alan

I'm determined to get ahead. I'm not afraid of hard work or of taking a few hard knocks. I'm not against climbing over a few people who get in the way. This job means a lot to me. I want to be somebody. I can't be satisfied with a mediocre job.

a Because you come from a working-class background you feel you have to get on and do really well.

b You've got the right idea. You can't put your own career at risk by pussy-footing around.

c You see yourself as a very ambitious person, is that it?

d What do you suppose makes you so determined to get ahead?

e I can help you with some tests to find out what your strongest skills are, but you've got such drive you are sure to do well in anything you try.

10 Rosy

I can't stay. Things are crazy at home, what with hubby off work with that crook back. What will I do with the holidays coming up? Help! Do you know where I can get sitters or something. I have to have some time for me!

a You'll really have to put the needs of your husband and children first over this period. He can't help having a bad back.
b Never mind. The holidays aren't for very long and I'm sure your husband will be OK soon.
c What is it you wanted time to do over the holidays?
d You probably feel that way because you've got used to having time to yourself and you think life should be a bed of roses all the time.
e You sound really pushed. Everyone seems to be needing you at once and there seems to be no time for yourself.

11 Kelly

We've been here for years. I was a kid in this area but you wouldn't know it. We don't have any friends. Anyway most people can't stand the kids. I guess five littlies is a lot when I call in on them. Anyway, I don't need to see people; I'm too busy.

a How often do you visit your neighbours?
b You're feeling pretty lonely and almost past caring.
c You probably don't have friends because you haven't made the effort to get to know the neighbours.
d Well you can't expect to have time for social chit chat with such a large family.
e I'm sure people like you and don't mind the kids as much as you think.

12 Doug

I can't get this child to sit still for one minute. He's making it impossible for me to cut his hair. I've tried everything and nothing works. What can I do?

a You should try being much firmer with him and insisting that he conforms.

b He's the youngest in the family and used to getting his own way.

c Have you told the parents?

d Don't worry; he will probably settle down soon.

e You're fed up with this child. He's upsetting you and you don't know what to try next.

13 Sandy

Well, as a student I'm just expected to do what I'm told, not rock the boat, just do and say what has been done and said for the last hundred years!

a You have trouble with people in authority and you don't like being told what to do.

b Never mind. When you graduate you'll be able to do it your way.

c You have to remember that your teachers are very experienced and it's their job to teach you what to do.

c You don't feel you can attempt anything new and it's really frustrating.

e Well don't you think they know how things should be done when they have been in the job so long?

14 Ken

I can't find my wallet! I think I left it in the car while it was parked outside the house and it's not there now. Oh! How could I? I had just cashed $300 for the rent! All my credit cards were in it too . . .

a What a shame! But maybe it's not really lost.

b You ought to know by now that you have to lock everything up and you can't trust anyone.

c How infuriating! You're scared you might have lost the lot!

d How long did you leave the car there?

e You have always been too trusting.

15 Mary

My mother has been sick, my father has left home and my sister has a new baby. I've been looking after all of them as well as my little sister and I just haven't had the time to do that extra work.

I'm terribly behind and I'm really scared I'm going to lose my job.

a You've been so busy propping up your family that you've let your own commitments go and now you're really worried.

b How much work are you behind in?

c It's right and proper that you put your family first; you may just have to lose your job.

d I'm sure you'll catch up in time. It can't be that bad.

e You wouldn't get so behind if you organised yourself better.

Analyze your responses by filling in the following table according to the instructions:

ITEM	RESPONSE				
	I	II	III	IV	V
1	b	d	c	a	e
2	c	a	b	e	d
3	a	c	e	d	b
4	d	e	a	b	c
5	e	b	d	c	a
6	d	b	c	e	a
7	c	e	d	a	b
8	e	d	a	b	c
9	b	a	e	d	c
10	a	d	b	c	e
11	d	c	e	a	b
12	a	b	d	c	e
13	c	a	b	e	d
14	b	e	a	d	c
15	c	e	d	b	a
Totals					

Look along the row from Item 1. Ring the letter in the first row which corresponds to your response for Item 1.

For Item 2 do the same in the second row and so on, repeating this process for each item.

Add up the total number of circles you have made in each column and write the totals at the bottom of each column.

Notice which column most of your responses were in. The columns represent the following styles:

I – Judgemental/evaluative/moralistic

II – Interpretive/explanatory/analyzing

III – Supportive/soothing/sympathetic/reassuring

IV – Probing/questioning/information gathering

V – Empathic/understanding/reflecting/paraphasing

Did you find that you used one style more often than the others? If so which did you use most?

Five Response Styles In an excellent book *Reaching Out*, David Johnson mentions that Carl Rogers isolated five different categories of response which he claimed accounted for 80 per cent of all the responses made in face-to-face situations. He found that if a person used one style of response as much as 40 per cent of the time then the person was seen by others as always responding in that way and tended to be described as that kind of person. For example, people who respond judgementally about 40 per cent of the time tended to be described as judgemental.

He also found that people in all sorts of different situations – business people, housewives, people at parties or conventions etc. – tended to use judgemental responses most frequently. The second most frequently used response style was interpretive, followed by supportive, then probing. Understanding responses were least often used.

Think about your response style and compare your responses with Rogers' findings. Do you think your answers reflected your usual style? Do you think your way of responding matched the way you thought you were or the way you want to be, that is, your self-perception and your values and intentions? Some styles are more helpful than others. If you want to communicate goodwill and be helpful to other people or to convey to them your wish to understand and to share in their experience, but your most common responses were judgemental, you might want to ask yourself whether people do confide in you readily or whether they shy away from sharing feelings for fear of being judged.

If you ringed mainly probing responses you could ask some of your friends if they feel you put them through the third degree. Do they often feel interrogated? You may think this would involve further interrogation. It is possible to phrase a request for information in a self-disclosing way rather than a probing way: 'I am wondering if ...' or 'I am concerned to find out if I come across to you as ...' You will see that asking for information by using an 'I' message is a direct statement of your own needs, whereas probing questions can put the other person on the defensive leading to a breakdown in communications.

The table on pp. 50–1 summarizes the intentions behind the five different response styles and suggests some possible effects, particularly when feelings are being discussed.

SUMMARY OF RESPONSE STYLES

	I Judgemental Evaluative Advice Giving	II Interpretive Explanatory	III Supporting Reassuring	IV Probing Exploratory Questioning Information seeking	V Understanding Empathic Reflecting Paraphrasing
RESPONSE DESCRIPTION	'I think you should . . .'	'You do that because . . .'	'Never mind, it's bound to get better.'	'When did you first feel that way?'	'You sound really happy'
INTENTIONS	To make a judgement on the goodness/badness, rightness/ wrongness. To tell the other person what he or she should/should not do. To put things right.	To explain the cause. To tell the meaning. To teach the other person.	To reassure. To minimize feeling. To soften the blow. To avoid intense feelings.	To seek more information. To tell the speaker what is OK or important to talk about.	To check whether responder understands accurately. To clarify what has been said. To stay close to here and now experience of speaker. To understand and share.
POSSIBLE EFFECTS	May create distrust. May be helpful when	Sets the responder above the speaker as wiser, more	Makes speaker feel more secure, less alone. May leave	Gives more information to responder. May	Encourages speaker to continue the

exploration of feelings and ideas further. Communicates acceptance and concern to the speaker. Communicates respect. Speaker feels understood, less lonely, more self-accepting, less self-deprecating, more aware of own value, more free to act appropriately when ready.

open up new aspects for speaker and lead to clarification. Moves topic away from here and now experience. May make both people feel safer. Intellectualizes conversation from feelings to facts. Moves focus from what speaker wants to say to what listener wants to know. May block the conversation and shut the speaker up.

speaker feeling not understood. Minimizes feelings. May indicate that feelings are temporary. May encourage avoidance of feelings. May give speaker false sense of security and reduce efforts for change. Shifts focus from speaker to responder.

clever and better informed. Gives information/insight – seldom leads to change. Intellectualizes the conversation moving it away from feelings. Moves focus from speaker to responder. Can help, usually doesn't.

judgement is asked for. Sets the responder above the speaker as more authoritative. Says to speaker 'I know more about your situation than you do and this is how you should act.' May put the speaker on the defensive leading to resentment, closing up, resistance, argument. Moves the focus from the speaker to the responder. Says some feelings are not OK. Leads to censoring. Limits communication.

Note: Often one response mixes a number of intentions and may fit more than one category.

51

A particular style is not in itself necessarily good or bad. Each communicates different intentions and each has a different effect on the conversation. Each has a place depending on the situation. From your own experience of the effect other people have on you, you probably have some ideas about the appropriateness of each response in different situations. Most of us don't share our innermost feelings with very judgemental people, and we tend to go silent when asked too many probing questions. There are times when we really need and appreciate support and comfort, but too much prolonged sympathy or support may not assist us to take necessary action.

Note that the first four response styles all tend to create distance between people. They also tend to move the conversation from the here and now of immediate feelings to a more distant, abstract and intellectual level. If you want to maintain a reasonable distance this is fine, but if you want more closeness and understanding you may want to practise a more empathic way of responding.

Carl Rogers made the observation that as a therapist he had found that the moments when a client was most open to change, or when the client did change, were those moments when client and therapist were relating on an equal and deeply personal level as two real human beings; not the moments when the therapist was making clever, authoritative, intellectual or interpretive statements.

It might be useful to think about this in relation to how other professionals respond to their clients or patients. For example, teachers often feel compelled to advise parents about what they *should* do, feeling a sense of responsibility for changing the way a parent relates to a child on the basis of their 'superior' knowledge. Think what effect this might have on a parent, on the parent's sense of self-worth and competence, and on his or her willingness to share feelings and concerns with the teacher. The parent may well want factual information, which can be very empowering and provide a more solid basis for making decisions and trying out new directions, but this is different from telling the parent what they should or should not do.

Similarly, if a friend confides in you about some complications

in their life, you don't need to know the answers to their problems or tell them what they should do in order to be helpful. Just feeling understood by you will be enormously helpful in itself.

Most of us are very good at the first four response styles; we use them often and with ease and certainly need no further training. It can be difficult, however, to respond with understanding, particularly if the other person's feelings seem negative, inappropriate or self-destructive, so these are the responses many of us need to work on, not in order to be counsellors, but in order to increase our repertoire, and to be more understanding when we want to be. The following couple of exercises should give you some practice in this area.

Awareness Exercise

Spend some time over the next few days becoming more aware of the way you respond in real life situations.

Responding to Feelings
Listen for Feelings

Practise deliberately not making judgements, not giving advice and not interpreting in situations when one of these would have been your normal response. Practise listening for feelings and asking yourself what feelings the other person is experiencing. Don't forget to note their non-verbal expressions as well as their words. Try to think of various different words which you could use to describe the feelings you see or hear the person expressing.

Feeling Words

Expand your vocabulary of feeling words and phrases by making some lists for yourself of different ways of expressing feelings. Don't be afraid to use colloquialisms or slang words. Keep adding to your lists as new words occur to you. Make lists for other feelings too.

anger	fear	joy
annoyed	afraid	elated
fed up	scared	on cloud nine
pissed off	nervous	bursting with happiness
furious	trembly	glad
wild	agitated	bouncy
resentful	anxious	on top of the world
irritated	uneasy	bubbly
mad	worried	jubilant
murderous	terrified	thrilled
seething	fearful	overjoyed
spiteful	panicky	delighted
_____	_____	_____
_____	_____	_____
_____	_____	_____
_____	_____	_____

Listening

One friend, one person who is truly understanding, who takes the trouble to listen to us as we consider our problem, can change our whole outlook on the world.

Dr Elton Mayo

Listening is more than just hearing. Hearing involves physiological sensory processes by which auditory sensations are received by the ears and transmitted to the brain. Listening, on the other hand involves, in addition, the complex psychological processes of decoding, that is, of interpreting and understanding the meaning and significance of the sensory experience.

It is quite possible to hear without really listening, as we all know. You have probably had the experience of saying to someone, 'You're not listening to me', and having them say, 'Oh yes I was, you said . . .' They repeat word for word what you have just said yet you realize that although they heard your words they had not really listened to or understood your meaning.

Effective Listening In order to know if you are listening effectively you need to consider what your intentions are and what effects you are aiming for.

Let us suppose that you want to listen to others in such a way as to develop optimal relationships, whether these be close personal relationships, work relationships or simply casual contacts. You might want also to be a person with whom others enjoy sharing their experiences, their feelings of joy, delight, grief, sadness, fear, anger, frustration, the whole range of human experience. Maybe you want to learn to respond more helpfully to other people as well.

Think about what you want to achieve through better listening.

Helping Others Suppose you want to be able to help other people, for instance a friend or a workmate who is worried, upset, or disturbed. You will need to respond in ways which help them clarify feelings and solve their own problems. In *Reaching Out* David Johnson reminds us that:

Perhaps the most important thing to remember is that you cannot solve other people's problems for them. No matter how sure you are of what the right thing to do is or how much insight you have into their problems, the other people must come to their own decisions about what they should do and achieve their own insights into the situation and themselves.

It is most important to be clear about whose problem it is and who is responsible, otherwise it's very easy for the helping person to fall into the trap of taking too much responsibility and playing the 'rescue' game. This is detrimental to both 'the rescued' and 'the rescuer'. It can undermine the other person's sense of personal efficacy and competence, increase dependence and place responsibility for decisions in the wrong place. People have to live with the consequences of their own decisions so it is important to be clear about personal boundaries and personal responsibilities.

So how can we respond helpfully in a way which allows people to be responsible for themselves and promote their personal strength?

Two basic things that determine whether you will be effective in this way are:

- your attitudes,
- your skills.

The attitudes you hold towards the other person are probably the most important factors in helping them. You could learn all the skills in the world about how to phrase your responses, yet if your heart is not in the right place these skills would simply be like pretty icing on an indigestible cake. As David Johnson says:

It is only when the skills in phrasing responses reflect your underlying attitudes of acceptance, respect, interest, liking and desire to help that your responses will be truly helpful. Your response is helpful when it helps another person explore a problem, clarify feelings, gain insight into a distressing situation or make a difficult decision.

Listening skills used by people who are non-caring, authoritarian or controlling, who do not respect the individuality and personal autonomy of others, who have false or hidden negative attitudes or whose intention is to manipulate and control for their own ends do not help other people. They are also likely to sound phoney and artificial and leave the receiver feeling uncomfortable and diminished. The critical question to ask yourself is whether the person you are listening and responding to feels understood? It may be useful to ask them directly.

How Did I Become the Kind of Listener I Am? So you want to be able to help other people and you are starting to discover how important it is to be an understanding listener. Maybe you are becoming aware that, like most people, your usual style of listening and responding may be positively unhelpful. It's important to be honest in your self-appraisal even if it's a bit upsetting. Remember, you can improve. Ponder for a moment on how you came to be the kind of listener you are. Consider how and what you learned about listening as a child.

Probably the most effective way of learning to listen well is to have the experience of being listened to in an understanding way by significant people. If parents and teachers listen to children in this way, then not only will they have a 'good' model, but they will feel good about themselves, and feel valued, accepted and respected as worthwhile people, and so develop a high level of self-esteem.

Burley-Allen puts it well in her book *Listening: The Forgotten Skill*, where she writes:

The way adults listen to children tells children something about themselves. Parents who interrupt their children, look stern while listening, ignore their children's feelings, or turn away when their children are talking send a message that what the children have to say is stupid or unimportant. This has a negative effect on the child's self-concept – an effect that lasts well into adulthood. As a result listening ability is hampered. Studies show that when people are anxious or worried about approval, they have trouble concentrating on what is being said.

> ## Self-esteem is a key to being an understanding listener.

It is easier to accept and respect other people when you accept and respect yourself. But if your self-esteem is rather low, do not despair; learning to be a better listener will improve your relationships with others and this is likely to enhance your self-esteem as well. It is a complex process and you can start anywhere.

Unfortunately most children receive a steady diet of negative teaching. A research study in which the verbal communications of mothers to children were analysed noted that most of the comments the mothers made to the children consisted of directions, commands and reprimands. It is hardly surprising that children learn not to attend or listen, since what they hear when they do is often unpleasant or unrewarding. Some common adult statements to children do actually exhort them to listen, but in a very negative and ineffective way:

Shut up and listen!

Be quiet!

Open your ears!

Listen to your mother and do what you're told!

Listening may come to be associated with negative feelings of discomfort and resentment. Perhaps it is better not to listen if you are likely to hear only nasty things. Note how acute a child's hearing suddenly seems to be when ice-cream or television is mentioned.

Think about how you were listened to as a child. You may like to run through the following exercise.

Your Early Experience

How did your parents listen to you when you were young?
Check the following:

	Mother	Father
Listened with complete attention		
Asked so many questions I felt I was being interrogated		
Listened with divided attention		
Listened reluctantly with bored expression		
Showed little interest		
Interrupted me		
Was pre-occupied with something else while saying, 'Hmmm'		
Lectured me		
Told me I was a chatterbox		
Talked non-stop at me		

How did you respond
to mother?
to father?

What did you say to yourself
  about mother?
  about father?

How did you feel?

How does this affect your present listening style?

What positive messages could a parent or teacher give a child? How might these messages be phrased? List as many as you can.
  I'll listen to what you have to say as soon as I have finished.
  I feel happy when you listen to me.
  Tell me about it.
  I want to understand how you felt.

_____

_____

_____

_____

Learning the Skills So far we have looked at some of the important attitudes necessary for good listening and at some of the ways we ourselves have learnt to listen. Now let us turn to the learning process.

Learning a new complex skill whether it be reflective listening, riding a bicycle or skiing, is not easy, particularly when it involves changing old habits. Learning can be made easier if the task is broken down into components or micro-skills.

The components of effective listening fall very comfortably into three main clusters of skills outlined by John Bolton in *People Skills*, these are attending, following and reflecting skills:

Attending Skills (being ready)
  Defining your availability
  Creating a suitable space
  Attending to immediate needs

Eye contact
Attentive posture
Appropriate movement
Eliminating distractions
Psychological attention

Following Skills (opening the door)
Invitations
Avoiding blocks to communication
Minimal encouragements
Open questions
Empathic silence

Reflecting Skills (keeping the door open)
Responding reflectively
How to make a reflective response – paraphrasing
Reflecting feelings
Reflecting facts and feelings
Reflecting silence
Reflecting themes – summarizing
Useful phrases
Language style

The aim of the above is not to present a precise model of listening behaviour to be copied exactly, but rather to develop in the reader an awareness of some important aspects of effective listening, and to provide the opportunity to learn about and practise some skills. You will then need to apply them appropriately to particular situations.

Study and practise each component separately, then put them together and integrate them into your own personal style and repertoire of skills.

Reflective listening may at first seem studied and artificial, yet we already use these responses quite naturally in some situations. You may not have been aware of how widely used these skills are nor of how other common ways of responding can block the communication process. The three clusters of skills are discussed in greater detail in the remainder of the section.

Attending

Attending skills involve ways of paying physical and psychological attention to the person who is talking, listening with the whole body and modifying the environment in ways that reduce distractions. People tend to think of communication as a verbal process, yet research indicates that 85 per cent of our communication is non-verbal. So attending, the non-verbal part of listening, is a very important part of the process of listening and responding effectively.

Defining Your Availability Clear statements about your availability can communicate caring and interest and a willingness to attend fully. You may need to set realistic limits and to arrange a suitable time to talk.

For example, a friend rings up and wants to tell you about a terrible day at work. Your husband has just come home, your children are ready for bed. Unless your friend is at a serious crisis point, you might say that you are unable to listen at this moment but will call later in the evening when you'll be able to give him or her your full attention. This shows more respect for the other person than trying to listen while doing other things. Setting both a beginning and an ending to your availability can be important, particularly when the other person is likely to be very needy or demanding, or your availability in time or energy is limited. If you are not willing or able to listen it is better to make this clear too.

Creating a Suitable Space If someone wants to confide in you about personal things, you could respect their need for privacy by arranging a quiet comfortable place free from interruptions. Seating positions are important too. Facing a window and looking into a patch of glare can make it hard to see the face of the other person and be very distracting.

Good places for talking are often very informal. The young children of one particular mother used to confide in her more than was usual. They would gather round her while she milked the cow. She would lean her head against the cow's warm side and the atmosphere was routine, relaxed and very safe. It was a quiet cow and the mother would listen attentively to the children and respond to them while she milked.

A counsellor I knew would sometimes walk in the park with a client. This seemed to be a natural and non-threatening way to be side by side and talk together.

Attending to Immediate Needs Sometimes in a situation of personal crisis involving very intense feelings it is important to attend to immediate needs first. This may involve offering the opportunity to be alone for a while, to take a walk, to move around, to breathe deeply, to have a cup of coffee or to do whatever is needed to feel comfortable and reduce anxiety. Sometimes talking about simple easy-to-talk-about factual matters, for example, the number of people in the household, where the person works or how long they've been there, is a useful way of giving an upset person time to collect themselves.

Psychologists and counsellors are sometimes so carried away with getting to the deep psychological levels that they forget some of the simple things. For example, a person might be desperately short of sleep, or may need a chance to be alone or just need companionship.

Good listening may involve helping a person become aware of and articulate some of their immediate needs and work out ways to meet them. Sometimes the simple question 'What do you need right now?' will open up some simple practical things they can do for themselves and pave the way for action.

Eye Contact Looking at the speaker softly most of the time expresses interest, attention, involvement and the desire to listen. Eyes wandering around a room indicate that your attention is elsewhere. At the other extreme, focusing too intently, staring fixedly or in a way that seems to probe, can be very unnerving and distracting.

The mother milking the cow and the counsellor walking in the park are examples of situations in which people have felt freer to talk (and felt listened to and understood) when not being looked at directly. So eye contact is important but you need to be sensitive about it.

Attentive Posture The body speaks louder and more honestly than words. A 'posture of involvement' is important for effective listening. In the book *Human Territories: How we Behave in Space-Time* Albert Schlen and Norman Ashcroft note that we can use each part of the body either to invite and facilitate inter-personal contact, or to break off, discourage or avoid involvement. Communication tends to be fostered when the listener is:

- relaxed and alert, but not floppy,
- leaning slightly towards the speaker,
- concentrating, but not menacing,
- facing the other squarely,
- maintaining an 'open' position,
- at a comfortable and appropriate distance from the speaker.

A relaxed posture communicates that you feel at home with the other person. Alertness or slight tension communicates that you are putting some energy into attending and trying to understand. A tight closed posture with folded arms can communicate psychological closedness, rejection, or defensiveness on the part of the listener. Leaning back in a chair can indicate lack of interest or even the desire to back away.

Comfortable physical distance between people is culturally defined. Factors include the situation and the degree of intimacy in the relationship. Normally about one metre is a comfortable distance in our society for non-intimate relationships.

Appropriate Movement Sometimes people learning new skills try so hard that they become rigid and immobilized. As John Bolton explains:

Appropriate body movement is essential to good listening ... the listener who remains still is seen as controlled, cold, aloof and reserved. By contrast the listener who is more active – but not in a fitful or nervous way – is experienced as friendly, warm, casual, and as not acting in a role ... The good listener moves his body in response to the speaker. Ineffective listeners move their bodies in response to stimuli that are unrelated to the talker. Their distraction is demonstrated by their body language: fiddling with pencils or keys, jingling money, fidgeting nervously, drumming fingers ...

Eliminating Distractions Your mannerisms can be highly distracting. They may convey agitation rather than relaxed alertness. Environmental distractions such as a blaring radio, a television, or a telephone ringing, can totally disrupt a serious conversation. A relatively quiet, attractive environment, rather than an ugly, noisy or uncomfortable one, is a great help in facilitating conversation. Be aware of how intrusions can distract both speaker and listener and ruin a conversation. If necessary look for ways to alter the immediate environment to make it more suitable.

Psychological Attention Psychological attention means tuning in and being really there for the other person, being aware of their non-verbal communication – posture, expression, tension level, energy level, mannerisms, eye contact and general demeanour. It involves suspending judgements, listening for themes, reflecting on what is said and checking that you've heard correctly.

To be effective such psychological presence must be genuine. Attending techniques accompanied by faked psychological attention or faked interest will not deceive the speaker. If your attention wanders or you are unable to be psychologically available to a particular person, at a particular moment, a genuine acknowledgement is preferable to pretended involvement. 'I'm sorry, my thoughts were elsewhere, would you tell me again?' or 'I'm sorry, I'm unable to concentrate today'. Your glazed eyes and other signals will reveal that your heart and mind are not there, but the speaker may well be confused if you pretend.

Strangely enough, improving physical attending is one way of improving your ability to concentrate and attend psychologically. The acronym SOLER is sometimes used as a reminder of the most important aspects of attending:

Squarely
Open posture
Lean toward the other
Eye contact
Relaxed

There are a number of ways you can experience and practise attending. If you are in a situation where you can practise with a partner, try the following activities. Practising exaggerated non-attending as well as attending can be useful ways of becoming more aware of the difference between the two. Reversing roles will give you the opportunity to experience how it feels to be on the receiving end as well.

Attending

Take a partner. Pick something to talk about. Anything will do, but keep to a reasonably simple and open topic, for example:

A nice thing that happened this week
A bad thing that happened this week
Something about yourself
About food

Decide who will be speaker and who will be listener to start with. Talk to your partner for about a minute. Change roles, so the speaker becomes the listener. Play both roles for each activity. Discuss how each of you felt. Move to the next activity. Be aware of how your feelings may be located in physical sensations such as neck strain. You may like to make up some extra activities of your own as well. Each activity should take about three minutes.

a **Non-attending**
   Speaker talks, listener deliberately does not attend: is silent, fiddles, looks away, leans back, folds arms.

b **Non-attending**
   Continue the conversation, this time sitting about two metres apart. Try different distances to see how it feels.

c **Non-attending**
   Sit back to back. Try to carry on a conversation.

d **Attending without responding**
   Face the other person squarely, attend carefully but make no response. What sort of response did you want? How did you feel without it?

e **Attending from unequal positions**
   Let the speaker kneel on the floor. Let the listener stand up. Try having a conversation. Note the physical strain as well as feelings of both people.

f **Attending at eye level**
   Repeat the above exercise with both kneeling down at a comfortable distance apart and with eyes at approximately the same level. Discuss the different feelings accompanying these two exercises.

g **Attending but responding with movements only**
   Attend well but do not respond verbally. Use head nods, facial expression, hand movements.

h **Attending using simple encouraging words only**
   Follow the above but occasionally respond with expressions of encouragement like uh-huh, mmm, etc.

i **Attending fully, responding as completely as you want to**

When you have carried out as many of these activites as you wish, take another three minutes at the end to discuss the exercise as a whole. What did you discover about attending and non-attending from both the listener's and the speaker's experience? Talking about a role play and any feelings it generated helps you to step out of the roles and back into your own shoes. Keep talking with your partner until you feel free of any uncomfortable feelings about it and you feel like yourself again.

Practice

a Spend some time becoming aware of how you attend to people in real life situations.
b Practise using some of the attending skills you have been learning.
c Notice how other people attend to you, what they do and how you feel.

Following

One of the most common aspects of poor listening is a tendency for the listener to lead the conversation and determine its direction. This tends to shift the focus from the speaker to the listener. This section deals with ways of following the speaker rather than leading.

As John Bolton says in *People Skills*, 'One of the primary tasks of a listener is to stay out of the other's way so that the listener can discover how the speaker views his situation.' Most people are too intrusive, too busy with themselves to be good listeners. They tend to rush in, interrupting the natural flow of the speaker by talking too much, asking too many questions, pronouncing judgements, and pushing the conversation into the direction they want it to go, sometimes aborting the speaker's message.

There are a number of ways of inviting the speaker to go on and indicating that the listener is there, willing, able and interested to listen. Essential to the success of any of these skills is always the listener's *genuine* desire to hear and to understand.

Invitations We may want to discuss a problem or share some part of our experience with another person but are unsure whether it is acceptable or whether they are interested, trustworthy, and so on. We often send tentative messages or non-verbal signals to 'test the water' and see if the other person seems interested and prepared to listen. For example, we may telegraph feelings of excitement, depression, irritation or pensiveness, by our facial expression, set of the shoulders, etc. This signal about our present state may elicit a response from the other person which we experience as an invitation to talk. Such a non-coercive invitation to proceed is a door opener. It may have one or all of three elements:

a A description of the other person's body language – 'You sound flat today.' 'You look very bubbly.'

b A verbal invitation to expand: 'What's been happening?' 'Fire away!' 'What's new?'

c Attentive silence. Eye contact, body alertness, and perhaps a questioning look, inviting the other to continue.

Having opened the door it is important not to try to drag the other person through, for example, 'You really ought to get it off your chest'; 'It doesn't do to bottle things up'; 'You know you can trust me'; 'Don't try to deny your feelings'. Pushy comments such as these can put people off. An understanding person and a good listener respects the other person's right to privacy, delivers an invitation, but does not press it.

Sometimes a person is ambivalent about talking, that is, has mixed feelings. Maybe they want to talk but are afraid or find it very painful. A useful way to deal with hesitancy is to verbalize it, 'It's pretty hard to talk about it'; 'On the one hand you'd like to talk about it, but on the other hand you're not sure'; 'It's hard to get started'; 'You're not sure where to start.'

Comments such as these indicate your awareness and understanding of the difficulty and say, 'It's OK to talk, it's OK not to talk, and it's OK to have mixed feelings about it.'

Avoiding Blocks to Communication Just as some responses on the part of a listener open the door and invite the speaker to go ahead, some responses close the door. Most of these are common ways of responding and people are seldom aware of their negative impact. They are often danger signals that say 'Beware, do not proceed'.

In his book *P.E.T. – Parent Effectiveness Training*, Thomas Gordon lists twelve typical blocks to communication. These are listed in the table below. He claims that 90 per cent of most parents' responses to their children fall into these categories.

Think about 'the typical twelve'. How do you feel about talking to someone who responds to you in any of these ways? What effect does it have on your wish to disclose your feelings to that person?

Notice that some of the typical twelve have already been mentioned in the section on response styles. You will recall it was suggested that these were appropriate in some situations. They are all used frequently in common speech, but some psychologists argue that the road blocks are never useful. There is no doubt they do have a high potential for blocking communication. They are particularly risky when used in intense, emotional, highly charged situations or where someone's self-esteem is at stake. I suggest therefore that they be avoided in these situations and reduced as much as is reasonable in ordinary conversation.

THE TYPICAL TWELVE-BLOCKS TO COMMUNICATION

1 **Ordering/directing/commanding**
'Don't speak to your mother like that.'
'Don't be so untidy.'

2 **Warning/admonishing/threatening**
'You'll be sorry.'
'One more remark like that and you won't go out on the weekend.'

3 **Exhorting/moralizing/preaching**
'I hope you realize that she is your best friend.'
'You should always be completely honest about things.'

4 **Advising/giving solutions/suggestions**
'Why don't you make more friends at school?'
'Moping around all day will only make it worse.'

5 **Lecturing/teaching/giving logical arguments**
'When I was your age I didn't think of dropping out.'
'You only get out of something as much as you put into it.'

6 **Judging/criticizing/disagreeing/blaming**
'That's a terrible thing to say.'
'You should be more tolerant.'

7 **Praising/agreeing/judging positively**
'Well, I don't think you are too fat.'
'But you're clever.'

8 **Name calling/ridiculing/shaming**
'Why don't you work hard like Joe does?'
'Lazy bones.'

9 **Interpreting/analyzing/diagnosing**
'You just want me to be with you all the time.'
'You'd like school if you worked harder.'

10 **Reassuring/sympathizing/consoling/supporting**
'Never mind; it can't last.'
'You'll cope.'

11 **Probing/questioning/interrogating**
'How long have you been smoking?'
'Why don't you like him, he's such a nice boy?'

12 **Withdrawing/distracting/humouring/diverting**
'Let's talk about something else.'
'Forget it.'

You may notice that a number of hidden messages are embedded in all the examples given. Some of these are:
'Don't feel that way.'
'Don't be like that.'
'I know better than you what you should do.'
'You're not OK.'
'You should be different.'
'Your feelings aren't important.'
All of these can and do undermine self-esteem, and can and do shut off open communication.
Some danger signals are idiosyncratic. These are particular

words or phrases which individual people react to negatively. Others are triggers for most people. Look at this list and check off the ones which are sensitive phrases for you, which put you on the defensive, trigger your anger, and block communication. Add any others that are particular danger signals for you.

'You always ...'
'You don't seem to appreciate ...'
'You're too ...'
'You never ...'
'You should/must/ought ...'
'You lack ...'
'You fail to ...'
'You are so selfish/confused/thoughtless.'
'Why can't you ...'
'Lazybones!'
'Don't be so childish!'

_____

_____

_____

Note that nearly all the communication blockers are 'you' messages, that is, a label or a comment about you from the other person.

Minimal Encouragements These are simple natural responses which are brief and to the point, giving minimal direction to the conversation. They literally 'en-courage'. They give the speaker the courage to continue without interrupting the flow of conversation. Examples are:

So	Really!	Oh!	Gosh!	Sure!
And?	For instance?	Go on	I see	Wow!
Yes?	Mmmm ...	And then?	Amazing!	Tell me more

These responses do not imply a judgement – they neither agree nor disagree with a statement. They indicate that you are listening and invite the speaker to continue. Sometimes this kind of response is overdone or used mechanically. Think of the stereotype of the non-directive therapist, who says nothing but 'Mm hmm'. It has been suggested that the 'Mm hmm' response

could be taken over by a computer! This response if used repeatedly is hardly likely to give the speaker the feeling that there is somebody there who is really listening.

Open Questions Questions can facilitate or block a conversation depending on how they are used. People often rely too much on questions. They use them too frequently and use them badly. Most of us are aware of times when we were bursting with news to tell, but clammed up completely or answered in monosyllables when someone fired a rapid volley of questions in our direction. This seems to be a common reaction to interrogation. When questions are closed, too frequent, too rapid, or focus on the listener's concerns rather than the speaker's, they are barriers to communication. Often the person on the receiving end tends to feel compelled to find answers or make decisions, often before he or she is ready.

To encourage and follow the speaker, questions need to be open, infrequent, well spaced, aimed at clarification, and follow the lead of the speaker. A closed question, such as 'Did you enjoy the party?' is like a true/false or multiple choice test question – it generates responses like 'yes' or 'no' or similar short answers. An open question, such as 'How did you find the party?', is like an essay question, an open invitation to the speaker to discuss a topic or expand on a theme.

One question at a time is enough. Several questions in rapid succession tend to reveal the questioner's agitation, poor timing or discomfort with the possibility of silence. Even psychologists and therapists are sometimes over-reliant on probing questions.

Bolton writes:

Almost everyone I have taught (communication skills) would have been a better listener if he asked fewer questions. Furthermore, I believe that most questions can be expressed as statements, and that doing so generally is far more productive in a conversation than repeated questioning.

Questions such as:
  'Will you be coming to stay for the weekend?'
  'What time will you come?'
  'How long do you want to stay?'
can be expressed:
  'I'd love you to come for the weekend.'
  'I'm wondering what time you want to come and how long you might want to stay.'
This can still elicit the information you require but in a less demanding style.

Empathic Silence Sometimes when people try using fewer questions they find they become very uncomfortable with the possibility of periods of silence. You can learn to become more at ease with silence.

Many people talk too much to be really good listeners. They are so anxious and uncomfortable with silence that they rush in to fill every gap in the conversation or butt in to prevent a gap occurring.

At the other extreme is the listener who sits for lengthy periods totally silent and unresponsive like a log of wood. Excessive silence can be read as lack of interest or boredom. Silence overdone forces the speaker into a monologue and can easily lead to day-dreaming and switching off on the part of the listener.

A good listener has the fine judgement to sense when to be silent and when to speak and is comfortable with either. Appropriate silence enables the speaker to set the pace and the listener to follow rather than to lead or dominate the conversation. It gives the speaker freedom to think, feel and express himself or herself without feeling hurried. It allows time to reflect and space to experience the natural ebb and flow of feelings. To be effective, silence needs to be a genuine and alert expression of attention and interest, of quietly 'being with' the other person.

Silence can be very special. Some of the most touching and most intimate experiences between people are moments of shared silence: 'moments when heart beats are heard'.

There are a number of ways you can reduce your discomfort. First of all, it is useful to remember that when someone is talking to you and sharing something important with you, the focus is on the speaker, not on you, the listener.

Secondly, it is up to the speaker whether they choose to go on talking or not. Raising an issue or a problem does not mean it must be talked right through or solved there and then. Many problems in life have no solutions and others take time. Your silence at the right moment can be experienced as a gentle non-coercive encouragement to further exploration and sharing, but you the listener need not feel compelled to keep the conversation going or guide the speaker to action. You only need to respond with understanding, if you can and if you genuinely want to.

Here are some practical things you can do or think about during lulls in the conversation. Rather than focusing on your own agitation you can:

- attend to the other person and demonstrate your attention non-verbally, with eye contact, alert expression, posture, etc.
- observe the other person, such as their expression, general demeanour, body tension, breathing, etc.

- think about what the other person is communicating and wonder about how it feels to be in his or her shoes.

Focusing on the other person tends to lessen one's own self-consciousness. Instead of thinking anxiously, 'I must say something to keep the conversation going', 'What can I say?', the listener can calmly think, 'I wonder how that person feels, I'll wait and maybe they will feel like exploring things further'. Bolton sums it up nicely:

The effective listener learns to speak when it is appropriate, can be silent when that is a fitting response, and feels comfortable with either activity. The good listener becomes adept at verbal responses while at the same time recognizing the immense importance of silence in creative conversation.

This absence of bossy interference is sometimes described as 'masterly inactivity'. Perhaps most important of all is the ability just to 'be with' another in an understanding or empathic way. As Lao-Tzu said, 'The way to do is to be'.

Refine Your Skills
Awareness
Next time you are in a situation where you want to be the listener, observe your own behaviour and note whether you tend to follow or lead the speaker. Do you encourage the speaker to go on, or do you rush in taking control of the direction the conversation takes?

Practise following
If you tend to lead, practise using some of the skills you have just read about, which give the speaker the opportunity to lead. How does it feel to be a follower? You may feel some anxiety or uncertainty about where the conversation is going. You have the right to set limits if you wish to.

Reflecting

The art of good listening involves the ability to respond reflectively.

Bolton

In a reflective response the listener paraphrases, or restates in their own words, the feeling or content of the other person's communication in a way that demonstrates understanding and acceptance. The listener attempts to check out with the speaker whether the message has been correctly understood.

As suggested previously, listeners reflect in two senses: they reflect upon or think about the meaning of the other person's communication, as well as being like a mirror which reflects back to the speaker the way the speaker's meaning has been interpreted. Reflective responding includes and extends the skills of attending and following already discussed.

Reflective responding does not mean parroting. Sometimes when people start learning to paraphrase they make the mistake of repeating the speaker's message in exactly the same words that the speaker used. This sounds phoney and inane and is very irritating. It may indicate that the words have been accurately heard but does not convey an intelligent understanding of the meaning.

Reflective responding can help people clarify and sometimes change the way they feel about their situation. Here is an example showing the difference between a judgemental response and a reflective response. The situation which triggers off the response is the same in each instance, but the outcome is different.

Responding to a Situation

Mary has had a bad day. First she loses her way when visiting a friend in the country, then she gets her car stuck in a ditch. As she's trying to get out she backs into a post and dents the back of the car. On the way home she is booked for speeding. She arrives home late and her father sees the state of the car and says, 'When are you going to grow up and be responsible? You're not fit to be let loose on your own. What the hell have you been doing? Can't you even get home on time?'

77

What would your reaction be if you were Mary?
    Burst into angry tears.
    Throw the car keys at him.
    Slam the door
    Scream at him that you couldn't help it.

_____

_____

_____

How would you feel towards your father?
    Disappointed
    Resentful
    Defensive
    Let down
    Angry

_____

_____

_____

Would it be easy for you to think about the necessary steps required to have the car repaired?

How would your self-esteem be? What are some of the self-statements you might be making?
    How could I be so stupid.
    What an idiot.
    Nobody understands me.

_____

_____

_____

Suppose the situation is the same. Mary gets home late, car damaged, etc. Her father sees at a glance she's been in strife and says 'Oh darling! You've had one hell of a day, the car, the speeding fine. You look quite done in.'
How might you react?
    Fall into his arms.
    Burst into tears of relief.
    Tell him all about what happened.
    Hug and kiss him.

_____

_____

_____

How would you feel about him? What would you be saying to yourself about him?

What a darling.

He understands.

I can ask him to help me fix it all up.

I love him.

I can depend on him when I need to.

_____

_____

_____

Would you feel differently about the whole situation/yourself/ your father? What would the differences be?

_____

_____

_____

_____

_____

_____

If so, why? The car is still damaged, you still have a speeding fine and you're still late home? What is different?

I would feel grateful that he hadn't criticized me, that he seemed to understand, that it is all right to have a bad day sometimes, that he was for me not against me, and that I could enlist his help and support in getting everything fixed up. I wouldn't be hating him or putting myself down as I would have in the first example. Is this how you would feel?

You will probably be aware that the father's response in the first example was a judgemental response. He made some good/ bad judgements – in this case mostly bad. The second example was a reflective response in which he summed up in a few words the key parts of what the girl had communicated to him both verbally and non-verbally, and what he thought she was experiencing.

The tables on pp. 80 and 81 show how to make reflective responses by paraphrasing and list some characteristics of good reflecting.

Paraphrasing

What to do:
- Attend to the whole communication.
- Imagine what the other person has experienced and is feeling.
- Translate that into your own words, paraphrase the message.
- Tell the speaker what you think they communicated to you.
- Be direct and simple. If you don't understand say so, e.g.: I'm sorry, I'm lost. Tell me again.
- Use a single word, a brief phrase, or a complex sentence.
- Reflect content, feelings or preferably both: 'Because of _____ you're feeling _____'.
- When mixed feelings, or separate ideas are expressed try to include them all in a paraphrase: 'You feel _____ but you also feel _____'.

Reflecting Feelings The reflection of feelings lies at the heart of effective listening. It is easy to reflect facts in order to confirm them. In a really good reflective response the listener paraphrases facts or feelings; preferably both. When facts and feelings are joined together in a succinct response there is a reflection of *meaning*, which represents a higher level of understanding.

Most people find it easy to focus on the facts or content of a message. We paraphrase these quite naturally when we interpret the meaning of an instruction, a direction, or other straight factual information, and repeat it in our own words to make sure we've heard correctly. For example, 'So you'll leave after lunch; that means you'll be here in time for dinner.'

Many of us find it more difficult to respond to feelings, perhaps because we experience some difficulty in being aware of them and in finding words to describe them, and perhaps, also in accepting them as valid. We are members of a society which largely denies

Reflective Listening

Good Reflecting:

- Sums up what the other person has said, making it clearer and more real.
- Checks out that you have understood and interpreted the meaning correctly.
- Reassures the speaker that he/she is being heard.
- Communicates acceptance, respect and concern.
- Is non-judgemental.
- Encourages the other person to go on talking.
- Is well timed – late after a pause, rather than early.
- Is concise, simple and understandable, e.g.: 'You're delighted,' 'You're feeling really upset'.
- Is accurate – reflects what the other person has communicated.
- Responds to the whole message – the non-verbal and the verbal.

feelings, in which rationality has a relatively high status and facts are considered paramount: 'Let's stick to the facts!' 'Don't let us get emotional and stupid about it'. Feelings are often seen as a nuisance, a weakness, best denied in the hope that they will go away and not disturb us, get out of hand or distort 'reality'.

> Feelings are real.

We often fail to recognize that feelings are an aspect of reality and need to be respected.

Problems with feelings can take two different forms. We can be blind to them and blinded by them. Being blind to our emotions can come about through believing that they are not justified, that is, believing that it is not acceptable to feel a certain way and we should not have the feeling. For example, 'I wish Auntie wouldn't follow me around the house. Sometimes I really get furious when she is all the time breathing down my neck, but I shouldn't feel annoyed because she's such a sweet old lady and she does her best'.

Feelings we believe we shouldn't have are often denied and blocked from our awareness. Parental messages to children are often instructions that reinforce the blocking of feelings. 'Don't be jealous, he's a lovely baby brother, we all love him and you must love him too.' 'Stop being so scared.' 'Don't cry, it didn't hurt that much.' 'Don't feel that way'.

Sometimes we are not blind to our feelings but blinded by them; we experience ourselves as being swamped by feelings and unable to think clearly. At such times we feel dangerously out of control and unable to direct our own destiny. Reflective listening helps in both cases. When people talk about a problem, the reflection of feelings helps them to understand their own emotions and thereby move towards a solution to the problem. Feelings are the energizing force that helps us sort out information, organize it, and use it effectively as we shape and implement relevant action. The danger for the listener is in becoming too probing for facts and forgetting the importance of feelings.

Ginnott puts it well: 'From a mirror we want an image, not a sermon'. The function of an emotional mirror is to reflect the feeling without distortion. 'You wish he'd just go back where he came from.' 'You feel pretty scared about taking on this extra responsibility.' 'You feel quite ecstatic about the recent turn of events'. Feelings that are out in the open, clearly named and accepted can be faced and dealt with and fully experienced. They are part of the experience of a whole person. When bits are denied, unrecognized and pushed underground, that person is less complete and less able to live life fully. Bolton writes:

When listening does not encourage disclosures of feeling, we tend to miss the speaker's personal reaction to events . . . joy, sorrow, frustration, anger, grief, ambivalence, and so on . . . we miss the uniqueness of the other person . . .

Feelings are often not communicated clearly. They may be masked and so may be difficult for the listener to pick up and reflect. Sometimes too the listener's own feelings get in the way. Practice is usually needed to become skilled in responding to feelings.

Sometimes it is hard to know what other people are feeling. They are likely to be experiencing a range of different things. Ask yourself, 'What are the principal feelings?' Here are some guidelines to follow:

a **Focus on feeling words**
   Alert yourself to picking up the words another person uses to describe their feelings, e.g. 'I am so cross with myself for being so careless as to lose my wallet'.

b **Look for clues in the overall content**
   'I spent hours yesterday going over and over what had gone wrong.' What might this person be feeling? Upset? Concerned? Anxious? Despairing? Confused? Frustrated?

c **Observe body language**

Pick up the hints. We communicate far more by body language than by words. Most people can read body messages far more accurately than they realize, yet taken out of context a particular gesture or facial expression may be highly ambiguous. A person's silent language can be misinterpreted. A frown can mean anger or it can mean the person is thinking deeply. A laugh can mean ridicule, it can mean joy or it can be an attempt to cover up sadness. Feelings are expressed both verbally and non-verbally, as is a person's way of coping with feelings. Try to be aware of the feelings and the feelings about the feelings. For example, 'You're feeling pretty upset but you don't want to show it'. Sometimes the verbal and non-verbal messages are incongruent. You can reflect both messages, for example, 'You're saying it's bad news yet you are laughing. What's the story?'

d **Put yourself in the other person's shoes**

Try to imagine how you would feel if you were the other person. This requires all you have in the way of imagination and understanding. The more life experience you have, and the more you are aware of and open to your own feelings, the more empathic you will be. Remember, it is only a guess, albeit an informed one. Don't be too definite or dogmatic. Be reasonably tentative and check out the accuracy of your understanding. If you are wrong the other person will most likely put you right.

People sometimes feel that reflecting feelings and so encouraging a person to talk is tantamount to agreeing with them. They worry that they may reinforce and intensify the feelings and thus incite the person to act without recourse to reason, perhaps dangerously. Neither of these things seem to happen. In fact, the reverse is usually true.

Suppose a child is angry and raises his arm to hit another child or an adult. Experienced therapists know that if that anger is verbally accepted and reflected, for example, 'You are just so cross with Bill you feel like hitting him', the arm will most likely fall and the child will nod sadly, relieved at being accepted and understood. When anger is accepted and can be talked about there is often a movement to a deeper level where the underlying feelings of hurt and loss are experienced. Adults are much the same.

Expressing feelings verbally and having them accepted and understood usually means less need to act them out impulsively. Suppressing feelings locks them away. They are out of conscious awareness and the person's ability to deal with their situation and control it effectively is reduced.

Reflecting Facts and Feelings Feelings usually occur in response to facts or events, so a reflecting response which includes both feelings and facts helps tie the two together and comes closer to the real meaning of another's experience:

Event	I felt
I was not asked to R's dinner party –	rejected
You kept me waiting the whole afternoon –	angry
They said my book was superb –	happy
We had a terrible row last night –	sad
I couldn't fill in the insurance proposal –	frustrated
I had hoped to spend the week with you –	disappointed
I was not able to arrange time off to go skiing –	furious

To reflect both feelings and facts the formula: 'You feel . . . because . . .' may be useful, e.g.:

'You *feel* furious *because* they expect you to work three nights a week.'

'You *feel* uncertain *because* you don't know what is expected of you.'

'You *feel* anxious *because* you are not sure what is going to happen.'

There are other ways of expressing facts and feelings within the same sentence structure. 'Are' can be substituted for 'feel'; for example 'You are upset because you failed your driving test'.

Words like 'by', 'when', 'about', 'with', 'that' can be used instead of 'because':

'You are annoyed by the constant changes in the regulations.'

'You are happy about your new friend.'

'You are fed up with his lying.'

'You are glad that the clients like you.'

'You find it scary when you are asked to speak to the group.'

Reflecting Silence Sometimes people communicate silently. You can still reflect the feelings expressed. For example, sometimes in

a communication skills workshop when the leader asks if someone will make a statement to which others can practise a reflective response, there is complete silence. No one moves. The leader can respond reflectively by saying 'It's really hard to think of something to say when you're put on the spot.' There is usually a mass sigh of relief when this happens, many heads nodding and people looking pleased at being understood.

You can respond reflectively to silence in many situations – to a group of people: 'You're all worn out', to one person: 'It's hard to know where to start', or to a person's appearance: 'You're looking very attractive today'.

You may also respond reflectively with silence. You may choose to reflect another's feelings by mirroring their mood non-verbally.

Reflecting Themes: Summarizing Sometimes people talk at great length. If you have time you may like to let them run on for a while, then when there is a pause you can attempt to sum up. This can be a brief statement of the gist of the conversation, 'You're on top of the world', or it may be an attempt to draw the loose ends together and make sense of the mass of detail, 'Let's see now, your main concern is . . .' 'There seems to be a recurring theme that goes something like this . . .' Often people can't see the wood for the trees. A concise and accurate summary can present a new and clearer perspective to a troubled person and can be of enormous benefit. Important themes occur again and again. Don't worry if you miss them at first, you will most likely have many other opportunities to pick them up.

Sometimes a person who is very worked up will talk on and on without a pause, with a great mass of detail. You may need to stem the flow quite deliberately by saying, 'Now, hold on a minute, let's look at the gist of what you've said so far' or 'Let's stop a minute and see if I can sum up what you've been saying'.

Choosing Your Words When you respond you need to be sensitive to the style of language which is natural and appropriate to the situation. This may mean matching to some extent the style of the other person, provided this is not artificial or false for you. For example, in responding to children you would naturally use language they could understand. In a formal situation your responses would need to be formally expressed. In a more casual situation, or with a friend, your language would be colloquial or even colourful.

It is important to be aware of this dimension when responding to people from different ethnic or cultural backgrounds, particularly when informality might be interpreted as lack of respect. If such a person's grasp of English is poor you might also need to use simple words, a simple sentence structure and speak more slowly and clearly than usual (not more loudly as often happens).

Choosing appropriate words also involves matching the level of intensity of the feelings expressed. Most of us recall being deeply moved by something quite out of the ordinary, such as magnificent music, and the shattering experience of having someone respond, 'It's pretty, isn't it?' A reflective response that is either a watered down or a grossly overstated version of the speaker's message fails to communicate real understanding. When making your lists of feeling words, group them in terms of strong, mild, or weak intensity to increase your repertoire.

Sometimes it is difficult to know how to start a reflective response. Since it is impossible to completely share another person's experience, the best we can do is to make a tentative approximation as to what we think the other person is thinking and feeling. We can aim at least to communicate our desire to understand and our willingness to be corrected. Here are some suggestions about phrasing a reflective response.

Useful Phrases: When you think you understand the other person accurately, you may find these phrases useful:

It seems to you that _____

You feel _____

In your experience _____

From where you stand _____

You're _____ (identify the feeling: sad, angry, overjoyed)

You believe _____

You mean _____

In other words _____

When you are less sure about what feelings the other person is expressing, these more tentative phrases might help you get started:

Let me see if I understand; you feel _____

I get the impression that you _____

_____ is that what you mean?

Do you feel a bit _____

Maybe I'm wrong but it seems _____

Is it possible that _____

Maybe it seems to you _____
Maybe you feel _____
Perhaps you're _____
You seem to be feeling _____
From where I stand it seems that you _____
It appears to you _____

These phrases can help you sum up the gist of a conversation:

Now let's see, you _____
One theme you keep coming back to seems to be

_____

Your main concern seems to be that _____
I've been mulling over what you've said and there seems to be a
pattern _____
Let's see if I've understood you correctly _____

Paraphrasing Practice

Here are some brief examples. Try forming a paraphrase then try
making up some more examples for yourself.

Peter: I could have clobbered Jim. He criticized me in
                front of the whole office. I felt so stupid. It was
                awful.

Paraphrase: You were furious at Jim for belittling you in front of
                your staff.

Instructor: This is the most wonderful team I've ever had. They
                are so enthusiastic about everything we do. I just
                look forward to every day.

Paraphrase: _____

Accountant: My sister's husband has just left home. She's left
                with three little children and she's very upset. My
                mother wants me to go and stay with her. I can't
                see how I can possibly do that and do justice to my
                job.

Paraphrase: _____

Teenager: I'd rather go window shopping than go to school. School's a real bore.

Paraphrase: _____

Friend: Yesterday a koala visited the big tree in my garden. I watched him for about an hour swaying around at the very top of the tree in the gale. I rushed around with the camera and took lots of photos.

Paraphrase: _____

Writer: Time's running out. I want to get my writing finished so that I can relax for a week before going back to work, but it's taking longer than I expected.

Paraphrase: _____

Patient: Now that I'm finally here I don't know where to start. It all seems so silly now. And I'm going to cry. I know I am.

Paraphrase: _____

Graduate: I did everything that was suggested to try to cope with being unemployed but I still got terribly miserable and depressed. I couldn't help feeling there must be something wrong with me even though I had been warned about loss of confidence.

Paraphrase: _____

Father: My son is doing his second year as an apprentice. He's always wanted to be a plumber, and now all of a sudden he wants to give it up. I can't understand it when he has only a little longer to go before finishing.

Paraphrase: _____

To help you form reflective responses to these statements ask yourself, 'What is the person feeling?' There is no one perfect way to respond, but many ways you could paraphrase well to really pick up the feelings. Aim to be as succinct as possible.

More Practice

a Try reflective listening with a friend. Take it in turns to practise, one to make a brief statement and the other to respond with a paraphrase. You can check with the speaker to see how your response came off. Remember one of the best tests of a good paraphrase is whether the other person feels under-stood.

If you have access to video equipment you could record your practice session, then replay it watching the body language as well as listening to the words. Stop the tape whenever either of you wants to comment on how you were feeling or what you were thinking about. As the listener, were you attending to your friend? Were you being critical or judgemental (or thinking about something else)? Did your friend feel understood?

Play around with this exercise trying out different possible responses until you are both happy with the outcome. Don't be too deadly serious about trying to be perfect. There are many ways to skin a cat. Remember to keep your responses brief, simple and as natural as possible.

b Practise reflecting feelings in a real life situation by para-phrasing. See how it goes and how the other person reacts. Be careful not to overdo it. You don't want to sound like a psychologist.

Some Questions

What Should I Do When Reflective Listening Doesn't Work? Most people feel a bit embarrassed and awkward when they first experiment with this way of responding. They feel self-conscious and think they will sound phoney and stupid, and that it won't work anyway.

Any new skill feels unnatural and artificial at first until it becomes integrated into the user's own personal style. It is helpful to practise reflective listening in a small group with at least one person who is familiar with the skill. You will probably be sur-prised to find how natural good paraphrasing sounds. People learning reflective listening in a group often complain bitterly about how terrible it would sound in everyday life, and all the while the group leader is reflecting back the feelings being expressed. Suddenly, someone in the group will realize and will exclaim in amazement that the leader has been listening reflectively for the last few minutes and no one even noticed; they just went on venting their feelings.

People learning reflective listening usually become very enthusiastic about the results, but sometimes they try it and it doesn't work. If this happens to you check the following possible reasons:

1 **You were not really listening reflectively.** One student reported that reflective listening was a condescending putdown and it didn't work. When asked to give a specific example

she said that her husband had fallen off a horse and her response when he told her about it was, 'I told you you were too old to go riding.' She believed she was using reflective listening! She had not realized how judgemental her statement was. No wonder her husband was defensive.

2 **You were not using reflective listening skilfully.** Being a beginner you might be 'parroting' what the other person said rather than putting it in your own words. This can sound like a robot rather than like a person who really understands and cares. When I first started learning this skill and was practising on my daughter, her reply was, 'I just said that, you dumbie!' Beware of overusing the skill; it can become irritating.

3 **You used reflective listening inappropriately.** Refer to p. 99, 'When Is Reflective Listening Inappropriate?'.

4 **You didn't really want to know how the other person was feeling.** You might not have been aware of this at the time. Perhaps you hold the unrealistic belief that you 'ought to' be able to listen to other people and respond to their needs at all times.

What Are the Most Common Mistakes? Reflective listening can go wrong in a number of other ways. If it doesn't seem to be going right for you, check the following list of 'don'ts' to see if you are making any of these common mistakes. You may think of other pitfalls.

Judgemental comments
Taking sides
Defensive responses
Inappropriate use of sympathy
Too many questions
Use of closed, inappropriate or irrelevant questions
Clichés
Too many lazy or inadequate responses (e.g. uh huh!)
Long windedness
Inaccurate responses

Patronizing or placating responses
Unsolicited advice
Responses that imply superiority or condescension
Responses indicating rejection or disrespect
Interpreting or playing 'psychologist'
Pretending to understand
'Parroting'
Talking too much
Jumping in too quickly
Letting the other ramble on
Responding to content and missing the feelings
Defusing or undercutting
Responding only to words, missing the body language
Responding with words only, forgetting to use body language
Overstating

How Do I Know if I Am Listening Effectively? As you try out these skills you will know if other people find you understanding and helpful by whether they talk with you about real, personal issues and share with you their joys and woes and occasionally their intimate feelings.

When a good reflective listening response is 'spot-on' the person will usually respond with 'right', 'exactly', 'yes, and . . .' They may nod affirmatively and continue talking, sometimes after a short, meditative pause and often with more depth of feeling and insight. Sometimes a paraphrase might be slightly inaccurate. This is usually not a disaster, particularly if a good relationship is already established. Often the speaker will say, 'No. It's not like that, it's more that I feel . . . and . . .' Misunderstandings will be corrected and the conversation will flow comfortably on.

In some situations, for example, in a group or in everyday life if you know the speaker well enough, you could ask for feedback about your listening style – did you come across as understanding? Often when people do feel understood they are so delighted they tell you without being asked.

Alternatively, the speaker may indicate that he or she doesn't feel understood by a puzzled look, by changing the direction of the conversation, by becoming more factual, more superficial or even abruptly cutting the conversation. One advantage of learning in a group or practising with a friend is that other people can tell you if they feel you are not listening effectively or are probing or giving advice.

When To Use Reflective Listening? Reflective listening is effective in many situations. Here are some suggestions about when to use it:

1 **When a person is conveying a message with some emotional content.** This is so particularly when strong feelings are involved or the person has a problem. It is appropriate to listen reflectively to people who are angry, excited, joyful, confused, upset, sad, etc.; whenever you genuinely wish to help another explore his or her feelings. It usually helps the person to clarify what it's all about and to arrive at his or her own best solution if a problem exists.

Often a person with a problem is not seeking a solution but simply wants to unburden themselves and explore some of the feelings with an understanding friend. It's great if the listener can feel comfortable with an unsolved or insoluble problem and realize the value for the other of simply being understood without being pushed to seek solutions. Some problems have no satisfactory solutions, for others time is needed before the best solution becomes clear. Unfortunately listeners often become impatient and frustrated. There is a terrible tendency to try to precipitate decisive action. Remember the phrase 'masterly inactivity'.

2 **During a direct mutual conversation.** In this situation both participate as speaker and listener. Neither person takes either role exclusively, but a natural switching of modes occurs. Reflective listening is highly appropriate and a very rich and profound conversation can take place.

3 **When the other person is making an indirect statement.** Sometimes a person hides the real message and speaks in some veiled way when feelings or needs are difficult to express.

Reflective listening can help the person feel safe enough to uncover the real point. For example, 'The spots on my hands are getting bigger. Mary Smith had some that were skin cancers'. The listener could put the unspoken feelings into words, 'You're worried that your spots might be serious'.

4 **Before you criticize, argue or get upset.** Arguments often take off in the wrong direction. Anger and indignation surge up because a statement has been wrongly interpreted in the first place. For example, a woman said to her ex-lover, 'You intrude at the most inappropriate moments.' He thought she was criticizing him for being insensitive and replied, 'That's not fair, I don't visit you unless I am invited.' He had misunderstood her. Had he listened reflectively to start with, he would have discovered that she meant something quite different. The conversation would have gone like this:

She: 'You intrude at the most inappropriate moments.'
He: 'You mean I visit you when it's not convenient.'
She: 'No, I mean I am still so fond of you that you often appear in my thoughts at the most inappropriate moments.'

How often it happens that when a heated argument develops at some stage someone says in desperation, 'But that's what I said in the first place'. People often argue with each other without really knowing what the other one has really said. They may even be in agreement without knowing it. Reflective listening helps minimize misunderstandings.

5 **Before you act.** Valuable time and effort can be saved by paraphrasing instructions to check out the accuracy of your own perceptions. For example, staff representative: 'Now let me see if I've got this clear. You want me to write a detailed report setting out our objections to the new office structure and proposing a new structure.' Clearly this helps prevent wasting valuable time producing work which does not meet requirements.

6 **When you are talking to yourself.** We all talk to ourselves, sometimes silently in our heads and sometimes out loud. This is

often referred to as 'self-talk'. People may be unaware of how frequently they are involved in dialogue with themselves and how often this dialogue involves a massive use of the blocks to communication tabled on pp. 70–1.

Advising: 'Why don't you just forget him.'
Labelling: 'You really are an idiot.'
Moralizing: 'You should have known better.'
Criticizing: 'It's all your own fault.'

Listening reflectively and non-judgementally to yourself can be amazingly valuable. It enables you to tune in to your own experience on the levels of both content and feeling, to become more accepting and understanding of yourself, and to clarify what is really going on for you. Take time to listen non-judgementally to yourself! Just listening in an accepting way is rewarding in itself. It can also lead to increased awareness to yourself and of your current experience and to ideas about what action you need to take to care for yourself. Compare the following dialogue

Initial thought: 'You're feeling really edgy.'
Response: *You just feel you've had enough. You'd just like to shut up shop and go camping for a week or two.*

with:

Initial thought: 'You're feeling really edgy.'
Response: *You shouldn't let yourself get upset. You ought to be nice to them. How can you be so touchy? After all they've been so kind to you. What a rotten sod you are!*

It is important to give yourself permission to experience the feelings just as they are, however outrageous they may seem. If you are really upset it may help to write them down, but be sure you resist the urge to censor them and pretty them up. No one else has to read what you write. You'll be amazed at how useful it is to listen to yourself with understanding.

7 **When encountering new ideas.** Suppose you meet someone with a radically different value system from your own. It is easy to make a negative judgement and condemn the person

outright, without really listening to the way they see the world or trying to understand how these values or ideas fit into the context of their experience. This applies particularly to understanding people from different ethnic backgrounds with different beliefs, values and customs. It is not necessary to agree, but it is important to listen with understanding, acceptance and respect.

New and strange ideas may come from a book, a lecture, your work situation or from other people. Robert Bolton refers to openness to different ideas as 'intellectual empathy'. He points to the difficulty most people have in coping with ideas which are unfamiliar or unwelcome, or which create conflicts with the values they already hold dear.

8 **After being assertive.** I used to acknowledge that being aggressive would almost certainly bring forth a defensive response in the other person, but I believed that being assertive would not. I thought that if I phrased an assertive statement accurately the other person would automatically accept it. Along with others, I have found that it is not so simple. As Robert Bolton writes:

Once an assertion message has been sent and silence has been provided (to allow the other to think about what you said) it is almost certain that the person to whom the assertion was addressed will make a defensive response . . . It is most important to 'shift gears' and listen reflectively to the predictable defensive response . . . this shifting back and forth between assertion and listening normally takes place several times before the assertion is completed.

Reflective listening at this time . . . helps diminish the other's defensiveness . . . and constructive conversation can begin again.

The defensiveness-reducing power of effective listening responses is truly remarkable.

When Is Reflective Listening Inappropriate? The art of using reflective listening involves knowing when to use it and when not to, and accepting that it is sometimes inappropriate and/or impossible. When appropriate, genuine reflective listening can be a very rewarding experience. But at times it can be a burden. Let's not kid ourselves, reflective listening is not easy. It can be hard work. It requires considerable discipline and can involve you in the personal ordeals of others as well as their joys and delights. It means overcoming the normal tendency to make judgements, to be self-defensive, express your own views, etc. It requires maturity, self-transcendence, an openness to other points of view, and a willingness to be vulnerable to being changed. Because it can be so demanding, give yourself permission not to listen reflectively at times. Here are some guidelines about when reflective listening may be inappropriate.

1 **When you are not able to be accepting.** When you listen reflectively the other person becomes more open and vulnerable. If you are feeling non-accepting and judgemental it may be much less hurtful to be openly judgemental right from the start. Don't listen reflectively and pretend to be accepting when you are not. It would be more honest to say 'I find it difficult to be understanding about that'. Reflective listening used as a technique when you are not genuinely able or prepared to be accepting is a manipulative weapon – it is false and destructive for both you and the other person.

2 **When you are not 'separate' from the other.** Reflective listening involves being empathic – being able to stand in another person's shoes and experience the world as if you were that person. The 'as if' is important. If the boundaries between that person and yourself are muddied and you are so involved with them that you are unable to maintain a healthy distance, then you are likely to be emotionally 'triggered' by that person's disclosures and to find it impossible to listen reflectively. Nevertheless, the discipline of reflective listening may be an honest way of trying to establish a healthy distance and gain a deeper understanding of the other person's point of view.

3 **When a person asks for information.** The question 'What time does the next tram go?' is obviously a request for

information and a straight answer is required. Imagine how irritating it would be to have a reflective response such as, 'You want to know what time the next tram goes.'

4 **When you use listening as a way of hiding yourself.** Sometimes reflective listening is used manipulatively to shield a person from close involvement with another and from experiencing the intensity of the other's emotions. This can be a cowardly way of setting oneself above the other person and remaining cool and untouched. It is not part of a genuine honest relationship and is an inappropriate use of reflective listening.

5 **When you feel very pressured, hassled, or depleted.** It is important to be able to recognize those times when you are off-centre and your inner self is out of kilter. At such times you are probably unable to be a good listener to particular persons or perhaps to anyone. It does more harm than good to pretend to listen when you are inwardly unavailable.

You do not have to listen to any person no matter how you may love him or her. It is important to explain that you are not willing or able to listen right now, if that is the case. It helps if you can indicate another time when this might be possible or if you make it clear that you are not prepared to be available to them at all.

6 **When you suspect the other person's motives.** Sometimes people are not as genuine and trustworthy as we would like. When you have good reason to suspect that the other person is untrustworthy and is likely to abuse your empathic nature and manipulate you, reflective listening is counterproductive. It may simply encourage the other person to expand on a theme which aims to make you feel guilty or to encourage you to be open and self-disclosing so your disclosures can be used against you.

7 **When it is overused and artificial.** One of the most irritating characteristics of people in the human relations

movement or people who have 'discovered' reflective listening is the tendency to use it all the time and to use clichés. For example, 'I think I hear you say you are feeling . . .' Reflective listening is just one skill. It is useful but it's not a magic cure for all situations.

8 **When a person needs action not words.** Sometimes a person's experience is literally 'beyond words' and the kind of verbal responses I have mentioned may be quite inadequate. You will be able to imagine or recall situations like this. At times a big, warm understanding hug speaks more than all the words in the world.

Trust your own intuition to guide you and don't berate yourself if your response occasionally misfires.

Skills Are Not Enough

Up to this point the focus has been on skills, but skills or techniques alone are not enough. As Robert Bolton puts it:

Communication techniques are useful only insofar as they facilitate the expression of essential human qualities. The person who has mastered the skills of communication but lacks genuineness, love and empathy will find his expertise irrelevant or even harmful. Important as they are, the techniques of communication by themselves are unable to forge satisfactory relationships.

I mentioned that many years ago Carl Rogers identified three essential qualities that foster good relationships of many different kinds. Since then over a hundred different studies have supported Rogers' theory. These three qualities crop up under various different labels. Some of them are listed in the following table:

1 Genuineness	2 Acceptance and warmth	3 Empathy
Congruence (Rogers)	Unconditional positive regard (Rogers)	Standing in another's shoes
Authenticity – being without facade	Non-possessive love (Bolton)	Sensitive and accurate understanding
Self-awareness	Caring	Ability to communicate understanding
Self-acceptance	Respect	
Self-expression		
Sincerity		

1 **Genuineness.**

Genuineness means being real. Reflective listening is a useful skill, but it is not good enough simply to reflect others as from a mirror. The listener needs to be an authentic person with a solid core of self as well. Being real and genuine involves the never-ending process of self-discovery and having the courage to know and accept even those parts that you don't particularly like. It means being without facade and being able to express yourself openly and honestly. This does not mean violating your own needs for privacy or being tyrannized by openness. It is certainly not appropriate to be totally open about every feeling with every person in every situation. Being open means being able to share one's feelings appropriately.

2 **Acceptance and Warmth.**

This is a difficult quality to label. It is sometimes called non-possessive love or positive regard. It involves respect and caring, and love in the sense of concern for a person's well being. People flourish most when they experience real warmth, liking and affection. People want to be valued and appreciated for their own uniqueness. While we cannot always manage liking and affection, we can perhaps offer respect and acceptance to others.

Liking crops up quite often as a problem. For example, teachers often believe that they should like every child, but of course this is not always possible. We frequently do not like all the people we believe we are supposed to like or love. We cannot turn on affection like a tap. Being genuine means that we do not pretend to like someone when we don't. Our being insincere doesn't help anyone. We can be concerned about a person's well being and want the best for them. In this sense we can 'love' those we do not necessarily like.

Acceptance means being non-judgemental or neutral. Bolton refers to it as 'in-spite-of' love. Sometimes it is impossible to be accepting. Feigning acceptance is not helpful. Non-acceptance if it exists is better openly acknowledged as concretely and specifically as possible. For example, 'Your behaviour bothers me and I find it difficult to be accepting' or 'I'd like to help but I can't'. Try to make an 'I' statement about your difficulty rather than labelling or condemning the other person. Try to leave their self-respect intact.

3 **Empathy**

Empathy comes from the German word *einfühlung* which literally means 'feeling into'. It means feeling with another person as if you were that person. The American Indians refer to 'standing in another man's moccasins'. It involves a sensitive and accurate understanding of the other person's feelings. Paradoxically, while it involves a close identification with the other, it also involves a degree of detachment.

The other important aspect of empathy is the ability to communicate your understanding to the other person so that they have the experience of feeling understood. This is where the skills come in. It is often the case that people feel they understand another person, but they don't know how to express this feeling so that the other person experiences it. The skills of reflective listening offer some ways to communicate your empathic understanding.

When these three qualities are present, relationships of all kinds are enhanced. Children learn better, lovers and marriage partners relate better, friendships are more fulfilling, business relationships work better, people are freer, healthier, happier and become more mature.

Perhaps you are wondering whether you have the essential human qualities to enable you to relate effectively to other people. We all have the capacity for these qualities by virtue of being human. Sometimes they atrophy from disuse or become blocked for various reasons. Sometimes too, we really don't want to share another person's feelings. Life can be tragic and we are not always ready or able to hear about the tragedy. It is appropriate to acknowledge another person's pain *and* one's own limitations in dealing with it.

Learning and using communication skills such as reflective listening and self-assertion can help to enhance your capacity for genuineness, non-possessive love and empathy.

Care for Yourself! Be sure to apply these qualities to yourself as well. The focus in this part of the book has been on understanding and helping others – but make sure the cost to yourself is not too

great. Don't overdo it! Make sure you are genuinely loving, caring, accepting and understanding towards yourself.

People involved in human services such as social workers, parents, teachers, counsellors, nurses, doctors, are particularly vulnerable to burnout. They may have a strong orientation towards nurturing and giving to others and may fail to care adequately for themselves. Indications of burnout include irritability, low energy, cynicism about people, indifference to suffering, loss of confidence and self-esteem, and general malaise. Prevention is better than cure. It's *your* responsibility to care for yourself. Listen to your own body. Tune in to your own needs. Plan systematically for the specific 're-creation' experiences you need to help you retain your enthusiasm, energy and general well-being. This might be a quiet day at home, a weekend in the country or a day off work. Don't forget that there will be times when you are not willing or able to listen to another person's troubles. You may have to be quite assertive. Remember, assertion skills are about letting other people know what *you* need, expressing yourself, and standing up for your rights and about ways of protecting yourself when necessary.

The next part of this book, Self-Assertion, deals with some of these issues.

SELF-ASSERTION

YOU CAN LEARN TO BE MORE ASSERTIVE AND FEEL MORE CONFIDENT

DO YOU GO TO PIECES IF YOU ARE CRITICIZED?

DO YOU FEEL NERVOUS AND TENSE MOST OF THE TIME?

DO YOU FEEL YOU SHOULD ALWAYS DO WHAT OTHER PEOPLE WANT YOU TO DO?

DO YOU CONTINUALLY WORRY ABOUT WHAT OTHER PEOPLE THINK OF YOU?

DO YOU FIND YOURSELF DOING THINGS YOU REALLY DON'T WANT TO DO?

DO YOU FEEL TOO SHY TO SPEAK UP?

ARE YOU ABLE TO ASK THE DOCTOR FOR INFORMATION?

DO YOU FIND IT HARD TO SAY NO?

DO YOU FEEL IT IS SELFISH TO SAY WHAT YOU WANT?

DOES FEAR OF FAILURE STOP YOU TRYING NEW THINGS?

DO YOU THINK YOU SHOULD BE A SUPER PERSON WHO IS NOT ENTITLED TO MAKE MISTAKES?

Introduction

The importance of high self-esteem has already been stressed in part I of this book, where it was suggested that learning to act more assertively was one way out of the vicious circle of low self-esteem. Part III looks at the importance of assertiveness training and some of the skills involved.

Assertion is appropriate self-expression and is quite different from aggression, with which it is often confused. Assertiveness training is about discovering your own inner wisdom and power and learning ways of expressing yourself clearly, honestly and directly.

This book is addressed to you as an individual, but individuals live and work as members of social groups or systems: family, work, community, society. We are all involved in various degrees of unequal power relations in our personal, economic, social, cultural and perhaps religious lives. However, because change in one part of a system brings about change in the system itself, increased power within each individual is revolutionary in its potential for subverting the effects of authoritarian structures and relationships. Assertiveness training aims to undermine oppression on both a personal and societal level. In this sense it is political. It is no wonder our attempts to change ourselves sometimes meet with pressure to revert to old ways and maintain the status quo.

In his book *On Personal Power*, Carl Rogers wrote inspiringly about the human potential for change:

When persons come into contact with and own and accept their inner strength exciting new ways of living emerge. When they find the courage to make responsible decisions they begin to change their worlds.

It is important, however, to be aware that there are limitations. Some people are more able to free themselves than others. This varies at different stages in life and according to circumstances. Standing up for yourself has consequences. If you do decide to become more assertive you have to live with these consequences, so you, and only you, can decide how far to go. At times the consequences may seem to be more negative than you are prepared to accept, and you may choose not to be assertive in that situation. Make sure, however, that you are not just taking the easy way out. Remember too, that constant non-assertiveness undermines your self-esteem and this becomes a vicious circle. Learning more assertive ways of behaving doesn't mean you have to be assertive all the time. It means you have more choice.

If you are in doubt about whether to stand up for yourself or not, you might like to apply the self-esteem test. If you choose not to assert yourself, will your self-esteem be undermined? If so the price of conformity is probably too high. The goal of this part of the book is to help each person become as strong as possible in relation to the constraints of personal circumstances and social pressures. Choose the ideas and suggestions which are most appropriate for you. Even the smallest changes may make an enormous difference. At the end of the book is a list of suggestions for further reading, which you may find useful.

It is difficult to go it alone. If you feel the task is too difficult for you to tackle alone, don't give up. Join a group or talk over your particular difficulties with an understanding person such as a friend or a counsellor. Seek out the kind of help you need – this could be your first step in being more assertive and caring for yourself.

What Does Self-Assertion Mean?

Assertiveness is a word which has various different connotations, and they are not always positive ones. Before reading further about the way it is defined in this book, make a list of adjectives that come to your mind to describe an assertive person.

Is this the kind of person you want to be?

Read on further and check your own impressions against the following definitions:

The word 'assert' derives from the Latin *asserere, assertum* meaning to lay hands on, claim (*ad*-to, *serere*-to join).

Originally 'to assert' meant 'to put one's hand on the head of a slave either to set him free (or to claim him for servitude). The word was variously defined as:

to ensure liberty, grant, protect, bring into freedom, champion, take the part of, defend.

Present day meanings provided by the dictionary are:

to declare strongly, lay claim to, insist upon, affirm, aver.

In thinking about the meaning of *self*-assertion, try adding 'oneself' or 'to oneself' to each of the above definitions.

According to the dictionary, self-assertion is the action of asserting one's individuality or insisting on one's rights or claims.

Let us simplify all of this and say that assertive behaviour means standing up for your legitimate rights without violating the rights of others. It is an honest, direct and appropriate expression of feelings, wants, beliefs and opinions. Assertive people communicate an attitude of self-respect and respect for others. Both verbal and non-verbal modes of expression conform so the message they transmit is clear. Self-assertion usually results in an increased feeling of self-esteem and confidence and, furthermore, a good chance of getting what you want or at least arriving at a workable compromise. The same should apply to the person that you are communicating with and both of you should feel good about yourselves and about the outcome.

> # Being assertive does NOT mean
> # being aggressive.

People often confuse assertiveness with aggression. Being assertive does not mean pushing little old ladies out of the way, stepping on others' toes, offending relatives, insulting friends or demanding your own way.

Perhaps 'appropriate expression' is a better term for assertiveness because it describes the meaning of assertive behaviour more clearly; appropriate refers to expression that accurately conveys the person's feelings in a way that will produce the most positive results; expression refers to ways of conveying how one truly feels in a situation.

Assertive behaviour can be seen as the balance between aggressiveness at one extreme and submissiveness at the other.

Let us now look briefly at what is meant by aggressive and submissive behaviour and then at how these forms of behaviour relate to low self-esteem.

Aggressive behaviour is a form of communication in which you stand up for your rights but violate the rights of others or put others down. It involves blaming or attacking other people and so holding them responsible. Aggressiveness is often the result of a build-up of anxiety or anger caused by submissiveness. The person's emotional thermometer rises to a point where they explode at the slightest provocation. They may also respond too vigorously, or 'come on too strong' making a deep and negative impression and provoking a defensive reaction in others. This may create distance or disrupt relationships. The intention of aggressive behaviour is to dominate, humiliate and control.

Sometimes people who are learning to be assertive unintentionally act aggressively. You can learn to distinguish clearly between these responses by trial and error and by listening carefully to how other people respond to your assertiveness. The section on listening skills may help you with this.

Submissive behaviour is a form of communication which allows one person's rights to be violated by another. This can occur when you fail to assert yourself, either:

1 when another person *deliberately* tries to dominate or control you thereby infringing your personal rights, or

2 when another person *inadvertently* encroaches upon your rights, because you fail to communicate your feelings, wants, or needs or fail to set appropriate limits.

Submissive behaviour is indirect, dishonest and inhibited. It often results in confusing double messages. Verbally a person may say, 'Yes, I'd love to babysit'; while non-verbally their body language says that they don't want to: their mouth is tight, eyes are averted, voice is either furious or weak and unconvincing and teeth are clenched.

Rather than communicating respect for others, submissive behaviour communicates deference and is self-denying. The submissive person often feels helpless, anxious and resentful of other people and blames them for not guessing his or her needs. Their intention is to avoid conflict or rejection, but the message is often unclear and the other person often feels confused and guilty. The outcome in the long run is usually damaging to the relationship.

Submissive behaviour may be specific to certain situations, but some people are submissive in almost all situations. If this is the case for you, learning to be more assertive may take longer and you might need the support of a counsellor or a group while working on the problem.

Aggressiveness and submissiveness are like two sides of a coin. Both are non-assertive and both stem from feelings of helplessness and a low sense of self-esteem. The non-assertive person

A COMPARISON OF SUBMISSIVE, ASSERTIVE AND AGGRESSIVE BEHAVIOUR

When your behaviour is:	Submissive	Non-Assertive Aggressive	Assertive
you are likely to be:	Indirect Dishonest Self-denying Inhibited Withdrawn	Inappropriately direct Self-enhancing at other's expense Expressive Blaming	Appropriately honest and direct Expressive Respectful of self and others
and you are likely to feel:	Hurt Powerless Anxious Angry inside Resentful A loser	Self-righteous Superior Sometimes guilty Dominant A winner	Confident Self-respecting Sometimes anxious Positive A winner
and the other person's feelings about you are likely to be:	Irritation Disgust Guilt Pity Disrespect	Anger Defensive Punitive Vengeful Hostile	Respectful Sometimes annoyed
and the other person's feelings about him/herself are likely to be:	Superiority Guilt Discomfort	Hurt Humiliated Put-down Inadequate	Self-valuing Self-respecting Positive

may swing between being quite submissive to becoming so resentful about being overlooked or denied that they suddenly overreact with an outburst of inappropriate hostility and aggression. Furthermore, aggressiveness and submissiveness both involve avoidance of responsibility. They both tend to foul-up communications, disrupt relationships and further lower self-esteem. The table on p. 116 compares submissive, assertive and aggressive behaviour.

> If I act submissively towards you
> I convey to you that you count
> but I am unimportant.
>
> If I act aggressively towards you
> I convey to you that I count
> but you are unimportant.
>
> If I act assertively towards you
> I convey to you that we both count
> and are both important.

The way anger is handled in each of these modes of behaviour also highlights the differences. When you handle anger submissively or passively, you keep quiet and cover up or deny your anger. When you handle anger aggressively, you blow up, blaming, punishing or degrading other people, holding them responsible for your feelings. When you handle anger assertively, you accept and take responsibility for your angry feelings and you are able to let other people know about your feelings when they occur and in a way which keeps everyone's self-esteem intact.

Assertive Behaviour and Self-Esteem

Low self-esteem leads to behaviour which is either aggressive or submissive. Similarly, behaving aggressively or submissively increases low self-esteem – and a downward spiral or vicious circle results.

High self-esteem makes it possible for a person to behave assertively, but similarly behaving assertively increases the level of self-esteem – and an upward spiral or benign circle is likely to develop.

To increase your self-esteem there are a number of things you can start doing. You can change your attitudes to yourself, as discussed in part I of this book. You can learn to listen non-judgementally to other people and so improve relationships as described in part II.

You can also change your behaviour and start acting more assertively as explored in this part of the book. You can work on changes in any or all of these areas.

The interaction between self-esteem and assertive and non-assertive behaviour is shown in the following diagram.

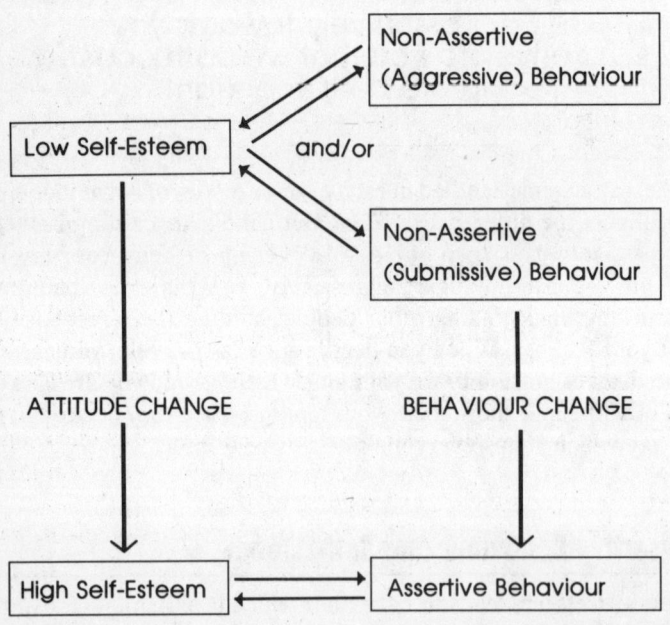

Why Be Assertive?

Being non-assertive, that is, being submissive or aggressive, has consequences. Some of these may apply for you:

- You are often taken advantage of;
- You avoid certain situations because you are too anxious;
- You find yourself doing things you don't want to do because you feel guilty saying no;
- You blame other people when things go wrong for you;
- You are afraid to act spontaneously because of fear of ridicule;
- You don't get enough time to yourself because you find it hard to tell your partner, parents, friends, or children what you need;
- You feel embarrassed and act ungraciously when complimented or praised;
- You miss out on important information because you are afraid to say when you don't understand what someone is talking about;
- You flare up and get angry and defensive when someone criticizes you;
- You feel helpless because you come back from a visit to the doctor or lawyer with your questions unasked;
- You repeatedly think of what you would like to have said or done after the opportunity has passed.

Being non-assertive has consequences for the way you feel about yourself, and the way you relate to others. It produces personal anguish, disappointment, self-recrimination and bitterness. It reinforces your feelings of being personally powerless, ineffectual and inadequate, or out of control. It undermines your confidence in your own potency, sometimes to a paralyzing degree. These feelings can manifest themselves in depression or anxiety, sexual problems, learning difficulties, or physical illness and a variety of aches and pains or rashes.

Many people have found that when they learn to be more assertive, a rapid positive change in self-image and self-confidence occurs.

- They feel better about themselves;
- People respond to them more positively;
- They feel they are being heard;
- They more often get what they want;
- Frustration, anger and resentment are lessened;
- They are more able to cope with conflict and arrive at mutually acceptable compromises;
- They no longer feel entirely annihilated by others' criticism and are more able to judge it objectively and use it constructively.

Of course assertion training is not a total cure for all ills, but in many instances it does have a very positive effect on a person's general well being.

Your Rights

One of the stumbling blocks which non-assertive people generally experience when they contemplate learning to be more assertive is their belief that they don't really have the right to have or to express their feelings, beliefs and opinions. This means that when they do assert themselves they feel guilty. Do you deny yourself rights that you believe others should have? Everyone has personal rights and has an equal right to assert them. It is important to think about your belief system and to question it.

Perhaps the first big step in becoming assertive is to assert that you have these rights and you wish to be able to assert them when you choose. Following is a list of my beliefs about personal rights:

1 I have the same basic interpersonal rights as others have.

2 I am happier when I appropriately exercise my rights, as well as respecting the rights of others.

3 Non-assertiveness is hurtful in the long run to me and my relationships.

The following sample of personal rights has been adapted from the suggestions of a number of writers on assertiveness, such as Manuel J. Smith in his bestseller on assertiveness training *When I Say No, I Feel Guilty*, Lyn Bloom and others in *The New Assertive Woman* and Robert E. Alberti and Michael L. Emmons in *Your Perfect Right*. You may want to refer to these books for more information.

These are not the kinds of rights which are legislated. You have them by virtue of being human. Even if you disagree with some of them it is worth considering them carefully. They provide a useful basis for discussion with your spouse, children, parents, friends, workmates, etc. If necessary make a list of your own that fits with your religious or philosophical outlook, but be sure you are consistent. If you believe in equality don't deny yourself a right that you believe others should have, or vice versa.

1 **You have the right to judge your own behaviour, thoughts and emotions and to take responsibility for their initiation and consequences.** This is the prime assertive right from which all others are derived – the right to be the ultimate judge of yourself. This right often generates much controversy, particularly from those who fear autonomy in self and others and believe that people must be controlled by external authorities.

2 **You have the right to offer no reason or excuses justifying your behaviour.** *Why* you feel or act as you do is your own business. You may not even know why, and it is not necessary that you do. What is important for you to know is *how* and *what* you feel and what you are prepared to do. You have the right to choose whether or not you answer 'why' questions about yourself.

3 **You have the right to judge whether you are responsible for finding solutions to other people's problems.** Each of us is ultimately responsible for ourself. We may wish to be compassionate and help others, but we help best when we help others solve their own problems and refrain from rescuing. Each of us has finally to come to terms with our own aloneness and to stand on our own two feet.

4 **You have the right to change your mind.** As human beings we are changing all the time as we grow from birth to death. As our experiences change, our interests, values, needs and wants also change. To be in touch with reality you need to be flexible enough to change your mind. It is often claimed that once you have made a decision you should stick to it no matter what – or if not, you must admit your past errors and justify your new choice. Your fallibility and the possibility that you might be wrong again may be emphasized. This is an attempt to manipulate and control you by undermining your faith in your own judgement. You have the right to make new decisions without having to justify the changes.

5 **You have the right to make mistakes and be responsible for them.** None of us is perfect. 'To err is human'. The idea that if you make mistakes you should feel guilty and atone for your errors is childish and unrealistic. It is impossible to be perfect. The harder you try, the more anxious you become and the harder it is to learn. If you aim for perfection, you guarantee failure. You cannot avoid making mistakes but you are of course responsible for the consequences. It is important

to teach yourself to feel comfortable and accepting about making mistakes.

6 **You have the right to say, 'I don't know'.** You don't have to know the answer to other people's questions or to know everything before you act. If you were to wait until you knew everything you would never act at all. People are responsible for their own actions but they cannot know for certain what the consequences will be. This is the human dilemma – the existential tragedy.

7 **You have the right to be independent of the goodwill of others.** No matter what you do, someone is not going to like it and someone may even feel hurt. You can take a stand with someone and assert yourself even if they do not feel positively towards you. People get frightened if someone threatens not to like them, but you will never be loved if you cannot take the risk of being disliked. The notion that we need the acceptance and approval of everyone, all the time, is irrational. It goes back to when we were small, helpless and dependent and felt we had to win the approval of parents in order to be loved and cared for – in order to survive. We were helpless then. We are not helpless now. We can survive on our own.

8 **You have the right to be illogical in making decisions.** Logic is a reasoning process. It is useful in black and white, yes or no situations. It is not much help in dealing with the ambiguous or the paradoxical, the grey areas of wants and feelings. But other people sometimes use logic to try to undermine your perceptions and prove you wrong. You don't have to find good reasons to support the way you feel. Similarly you don't have to deny a feeling because it seems unreasonable – yet we often do. There probably are good reasons for all the things we feel but we may not be aware of them, and our feelings often appear to be unreasonable and capricious. Accept and acknowledge the seeming unreason-ableness while still asserting the feeling. You can learn to be

comfortable in not knowing the reasons why, and to trust your own experience and intuition when making decisions.

9 **You have the right to say, 'I don't understand'.** True wisdom involves the realization of how little we know about each other. Sometimes we feel that other people 'ought' to understand automatically, without being told, what we need, why certain things are done and so on. We sometimes try to manipulate people into changing their behaviour by hurt or angry looks which suggest that they should understand by guesswork what is bothering us or what they have done to us.

10 **You have the right to set your own priorities.** Most of us have been brought up to believe that we have many flaws and ought to be trying to improve ourselves all the time, that is, if we do not try to improve we must be lazy or bad or worthless. But if you try to be perfect in anything (even in being assertive) you will be disappointed and frustrated. You don't have to improve your performance, graduate with honours, be more efficient, rise to the top of your career or make more money. Set your own priorities. It is your choice. It is often a great relief to decide not to be perfect. You can then go about the satisfying occupation of accepting yourself and enjoying just 'being'.

Other rights can be listed too:
You have the right to say 'no' without feeling guilty.
You have the right to have and express your own feelings and opinions.
You have the right to be listened to and taken seriously.
You have the right to ask for what you want.
You have the right to get what you pay for.
You have the right to decide whether you meet another's needs or not.

Most importantly:

> You have the right to choose
> whether to assert yourself.

Remember that these rights apply not only to you but to others as well, and they also have the right to assert them.

Why Am I Non-Assertive?

If you are non-assertive this is the way you have learned to be, although temperament plays some part as well.

In our society most women are conditioned to be submissive and self-denying and most men are conditioned not to express their feelings. Traditionally, the woman's role is to be compassionate and to serve and care for others; the man's role is to be competent, successful and strong.

These influences come from all areas of our lives. In the family we hear, 'Don't you dare speak to mother like that.' In the school, the most acceptable child is one who is neat, orderly, conformist and well-behaved, and who does not question or challenge authority. Many religions transmit the values of compassion, unselfishness, self-denial and obedience. Even at work most people are encouraged not to 'rock the boat'. Too much initiative is often seen as a threat to those in authority. Many people allow themselves to submit to incredible work pressures, which are often quite harmful to their general health, out of economic necessity or often a sense of duty and self-denial.

> Your SELF is a resource. As such it
> needs to be cared for and nurtured.

All around us are 'y'ought-ers' and 'should-ers' telling us how to behave. Sometimes just the mention of becoming more assertive is enough to bring forth a load of negative reactions and criticism. Many men, for instance, abhor the notion of an assertive woman, believing that she will be a dominating, emasculating shrew. If you want to become more assertive, it is important to realize that initially you may come up against negative reactions from some people, particularly those close to you. They might be frightened by the idea of your autonomy and, out of their anxiety, want or need to feel in control of you.

Try not to let this put you off or make you feel guilty about being assertive. Remember the difference between assertiveness and aggression, and remember that in the long run you and your relationship are harmed by non-assertiveness.

TWO VITAL TRUTHS

1 The only behaviour you can change is your own.

2 People are not mind readers. If you don't tell them, chances are they will not know.

Learning A New Skill

Learning to be assertive is not unlike learning to ride a horse or a bicycle. It is a matter of training. It is hard at first and may feel awkward and perhaps a bit silly. It involves taking the risk of making mistakes, but it gets easier with persistence and practice. It's a process which takes time and involves a series of steps. Some people learn very quickly, but sometimes it takes a long time and a lot of practice. This depends on many factors including motivation, readiness, degree of anxiety or confidence, expectations and predisposition.

FIVE MAIN STEPS IN LEARNING A NEW SKILL

1 *Awareness* of need for a new skill leads to motivation, e.g. wanting to learn to ride a bike for pleasure or fitness.

2 *Identification* of actual behaviour involved, e.g. knowing the actual body movements or words required.

3 *Feedback* involves trial and error, i.e. making mistakes, experiencing the consequences and learning by them, e.g. falling off the bike gives negative feedback, keeping your balance gives positive feedback and correct actions are reinforced.

4 *Practice* involves repetition until the performance of the skill feels less awkward and becomes more flowing and automatic.

5 *Integration* so that the new skill is adapted to your own particular style and behavioural repertoire. Choices are made about which learning to retain and which to discard.

At the beginning, any new skill feels strange and artificial. Feel free to make mistakes and experiment with different styles until it gradually feels more like you. It is important to start slowly, move in easy stages and tackle the least difficult situations first. For example, try being assertive with the butcher before you practise on your partner!

Your initial attempts at being assertive should be chosen for their high potential for success.

Success leads to success.

Close relationships which might have involved the non-assertive behaviour of one partner are sometimes affected when that person becomes more assertive. Initially it may be easier to assert yourself over minor issues or with people you are less close to until you gain skill and confidence. Move gradually into more intimate and vulnerable areas, and be sure the other person is properly prepared for the changes in you. Tell them what you are trying to do.

Don't expect that others will necessarily be overjoyed when you begin standing up for your rights and asserting yourself. It is a myth that assertiveness is instantly welcomed by everyone. Remember that stating clearly what you want, when you've not been in the habit of doing so, may bring conflicts to the surface, but this can be very healthy.

It is possible too, that you will be labelled as aggressive. Sometimes when women assert themselves men see them as aggressive because they are breaking out of a stereotyped role and are no longer silent or indirect. It could also mean that you are in fact being aggressive. People learning assertiveness often go overboard in their enthusiasm and are unnecessarily forceful.

Either way you will need to listen with understanding to the reactions of your friend, boss or partner. They may react defensively or with anger to your new behaviour.

Being more assertive will improve your communications and in the long term will lead to better relationships. Sometimes, however, a relationship is unhealthy in that it depends on the denial by one partner of their real needs and on the non-growth of that person. Difficult decisions between preserving the relationship or developing one's own potential may have to be made. Sometimes compromises over less important issues are possible provided your own well being and sense of self-worth are not at risk.

How to Start There are a number of ways of starting to be more assertive, some of which were mentioned before in relation to self-esteem. You can start thinking, behaving or feeling differently.

A good way to start is to ask yourself: What do I want? What do I need? What do I need to ask for? What is important to me and how can I make it clear that this is important?

Make a specific list of about ten of your own particular assertiveness problems. List the situations in order, from the easiest to the most difficult. You may find that the closer the person the more difficult it is to be assertive with them. This is understandable as there is more personal risk involved. Here is an example:

Shop Assistants: I would like to be firm about returning faulty goods.

Smokers: When people ask me very nicely if I mind if they smoke I'd like to be able to say that I do mind.

Accountant: I'd like to be able to say I don't understand what he is talking about without feeling stupid.

Friends: I would like to be able to say no when they ask me to lend them money.

Self: I would like to be able to acknowledge and enjoy my good qualities.

Mother: I would like to be able to say I don't want to live with her, without feeling guilty.

At this stage, don't qualify your answers or cut things out because they seem impossible. Later you will decide which issues you will assert yourself over and which not. This list is just for you and it is very important for you to be clear about how you would like things to be different.

If you have trouble identifying situations in which you need to be more assertive, look for physical symptoms of anxiety. Does your behaviour result in any of the following:

- headache,
- jaw tightening,
- heart beating fast,
- giggling,
- artificial nervous laughter,
- insomnia,
- tight neck or shoulder muscles,
- stomach cramps,
- backache,
- or other expressions of tension or 'dis-ease'.

Similarly, do you do any of the following things to avoid asserting yourself?

- blame someone else,
- explode in aggressive outbursts,
- procrastinate,
- withdraw and say nothing,
- feel flat or depressed,
- give in to please others.

You could keep a personal log book for at least a week to help you pinpoint specific situations you want to work on. You can make it in chart form like the example on p. 132. Refer back to it later when you are practising your skills. These lists and charts are all ways of identifying those situations that are difficult for you. It is easy to make general statements about changes you want to make, but before you start you need to know *specifically* what you do already, how you want to change, and what your goals are.

Managing Anxiety and Stress Many people initially experience considerable anxiety and tension when attempting to act assertively. Changing old familiar habits can be a scary business. If anxiety is a frequent and serious problem for you, take action to learn relaxation and stress management skills (see part I of this

SAMPLE LOG BOOK

Date	Situation	How my body reacted	What I did	How I felt	What I would like to have done and will try next time	Why I didn't do what I wanted to do
2/10	Accountant kept talking at me and I didn't understand him	My stomach was in knots I felt tired Developed a headache	Said nothing Nodded	Stupid Ignorant Frustrated Angry	Told him I didn't understand and asked him to explain it more clearly	Afraid he would think I was stupid
4/10	Friend rang up while I was watching interesting programme on TV	Shoulders tense and aching	Talked to him and missed my programme	Angry Resentful	Told him I was watching TV and would ring back later	Afraid he would feel rejected
7/10	Boss asked me to work overtime	Heart racing Flushed Shaking	Snapped his head off and answered rudely	Angry with him and myself Resentful Guilty Powerless	Told him I was not able to work overtime this week	Thought I should always do what others expect of me

book). You will also find it useful to become aware of ways in which you scare yourself by giving yourself negative and anxiety-provoking messages. Take steps to re-programme your self-talk so that you steady yourself down and set realistic expectations (part I will help you with this).

Don't forget that anxiety can be a sign that you are extending yourself and trying new things. It will gradually subside as you become more comfortable with the new skills.

Non-Verbal Communication

Messages are communicated both verbally and non-verbally. Your body and your words need to say the same thing. If your words are assertive but your body language is non-assertive, the messages conflict. The receiver may be confused but will most likely pick up and respond to the non-verbal part. So it is not just what is said, but how it is delivered that is important. People can pretend with words but the body doesn't lie. If you really want to be effective your body needs to communicate that you mean what you say.

Think of some of the following components of body language in relation to assertion, aggression or submission:
- posture
- facial expression
- gesture
- voice (timing, tone, volume, pitch, fluency)
- eye contact
- movement
- distance

Make sure you claim the other person's attention before you start so that they are really listening to you. Look directly at them; speak firmly and not too quickly; hold yourself well, head up and feet firmly planted. If you hang your head, avert your eyes, wriggle about and whisper, your assertive statement probably won't be taken seriously. If you point, stick your chin out or speak very loudly, chances are the other person will feel threatened and react defensively.

Developing Verbal Skills

A number of verbal skills will be discussed in the following pages, but open, honest, clear, whole messages are the best way to communicate in most situations. Other techniques are designed for specific purposes.

You need to be aware that some techniques bring people closer to one another while others create distance between people. It is important to select the most appropriate technique for each situation, depending on whether you want to increase or decrease closeness.

'I' messages, self-disclosure, and free information help people get to know one another better and, if they like what they discover, to become more friendly or intimate.

There are some situations, however, in which you may need to protect yourself and maintain an appropriate distance between yourself and another person. Fogging and broken record techniques are effective protective skills. They are very frustrating and annoying for the receiver but may be useful if someone is deliberately or inadvertently acting destructively towards you or is out to get you. They certainly do not endear you to the other person but there are some situations when this doesn't matter. If these skills are used with friends they are likely to lead to a deterioration in the relationship. Understand the effect of each technique and choose appropriately.

'I' Messages

> Try an honest 'I' statement first of all.

An 'I' statement is one in which you actually use the pronoun I to express yourself.

Making statements that start with 'I' enables you to communicate directly, clearly and honestly how you feel and what you want. If you don't tell others clearly, chances are they won't know. If you do tell them, you may not get what you want, as they have choices about how they will respond, but at least each person is clear about what is going on, and the possibility for negotiating a mutually acceptable outcome is improved.

Say your 'I' statement firmly and with conviction and make clear what you want, for example: 'When you act as if you are not listening I feel hurt, I want you to stop watching TV for a few minutes and listen to me'. If this is not effective try at least once more before resorting to other protective techniques.

Whole messages involve saying it all, including your mixed feelings, your feelings of anxiety about saying it, your fear about hurting others, etc. For example, 'I'm feeling both excited and frightened at the prospect of moving house'.

A whole message can also include a recognition that you understand the other's situation and feelings, even if you are unwilling to fulfil their needs. For example, 'I understand that you need this typing done today, but I need to take a rest break right now'.

'I' messages communicate your feelings directly, for example, 'I feel really angry about . . .' or 'I would like to . . .' The speaker takes responsibility for his or her own feelings. Compare this with, 'You make me angry when . . .' which blames the other person and usually brings forth an aggressive or defensive response.

Dropping hints about what you want, saying one thing and looking like you mean another, waiting for the other to guess your needs, stating only half the message are all devious devices which involve the other person in a guessing game. These games are confusing and usually misfire, leaving everyone feeling hurt, resentful, misunderstood and abused.

Feelings are real and need to be appropriately expressed. Persistent feelings don't go away by being denied or suppressed; they tend to build up and cause trouble. Both positive and negative feelings need appropriate expression and are best dealt with assertively when they occur. Don't assume the other person knows how you feel.

With this skill you can hope to achieve clear responsible communications, increased self-respect, and improved, less defensive interpersonal relationships.

Negotiation Towards a Workable Compromise People often ask what happens when both people are assertive and the other person doesn't agree with your assertive statement or request. Differences between people are easiest to handle when both people *are* assertive. An important step is identifying that a difference exists. Each person's goals and interests can be identified, imaginative solutions explored, and negotiation towards a workable compromise can proceed.

Self-respect for each person is one of the principal goals of assertion training; so self-respect is your guide in deciding what to settle for. When you exercise your assertive rights you feel better even if you don't get what you want immediately because you have said clearly what you wanted to say. If the other person is also assertive the conflict is out in the open and can be settled on the basis of the real issues, not in terms of who is the best manipulator.

If there is a real conflict of interests, and provided you don't feel that your self-respect is in question, offer a workable compromise. If the outcome involves loss of self-respect for you, there can be no compromise and you need to make this clear.

If you want more information about negotiation skills you will find very useful strategies in a book called *Getting to Yes* by R. Fisher and W. Urey. Negotiation towards a workable compromise is discussed in detail in Manuel J. Smith's *When I Say No, I Feel Guilty*.

Free Information This is a skill that helps you to be more competent in social situations. In everyday conversation, people give away many snippets of free information, which are simple cues about what is interesting or important to them. If you are alert, you will recognize these and then you can follow them up.

This skill bypasses the situation where you are worried about what you should say next and helps you discover whether there is a basis for a mutually rewarding relationship or not. It involves listening and follow-up.

Some people are afraid of social situations because they believe they are ill-informed on many topics and therefore cannot be good at conversation. This need not be a problem.

Use your ignorance constructively.

Make an 'I' statement without putting yourself or the other person down. Tell the other person that you don't know much about the topic but are interested and would like to know more. Ask the other person to tell you about their experience. Most people love to be invited to talk about their special interests.

The set of four cassettes by Guerra and Cotler called 'A Guide to Self Dignity' has an excellent tape on conversation skills in which using your ignorance is demonstrated.

When you have practised this skill you will feel less shy in social situations because you have something to talk about. You also make it easier for the other person by giving them an opportunity to talk about their interests.

Self-Disclosure This means assertively sharing information about yourself; how you are thinking, feeling and reacting. In order to like you, to be involved with you, to be your friend, or to love you, people need to know who you are. Everyone needs to be able to disclose themselves to at least one other significant person.

This does not mean that you should tell each new person you meet all your most intimate thoughts and feelings. You will need to assess what level of self-disclosure is appropriate and comfortable in each situation.

People who share how they are feeling are drawn together; people who stay silent about their reactions and feelings stay apart. Self-disclosure requires trust and courage and involves a willingness to take risks to build a better relationship. You may choose to stay apart from a person who is not worthy of your trust. Take your time to find out.

Being silent is not necessarily being strong. Hiding reactions through fear of rejection, conflict, shame, guilt, or fear of hurting another may be a way to protect yourself or the other person but can also lead to the pain of loneliness and isolation.

This skill helps you to feel comfortable telling the other person about yourself. Disclosure is reciprocal, so your self-disclosure sets in motion a process which brings you both closer together. When people disclose their inner selves honestly they become much less threatening and usually more loveable to others. We fear what we don't know. We tend to judge people by their often powerful and competent outward presentation of self, assuming that they don't have the frailties that we know in ourselves.

Negative Assertion Many people are unclear about how to respond when they are in the wrong. Manuel J. Smith in his book *When I Say No, I Feel Guilty* outlines a skill which he calls negative assertion. It involves assertive acceptance and acknowledgement of mistakes without guilt. For example:

Supervisor: 'You didn't do that job very well.'
Worker: 'You're right, I didn't handle that well at all.'

Supervisor: 'And you left some of it out.'
Worker: 'Yes, I've noticed that too.'

Remember, you don't have to feel guilty, ask forgiveness or deny your mistakes. Others may imply that you 'should' feel guilty but you do not have to accept this. It is all right to make mistakes, and you can learn from them. In fact it is very difficult to learn anything new without making some mistakes.

Negative assertion allows you to feel more comfortable about mistakes or flaws in your own behaviour without feeling defensive or anxious or resorting to denial. It reduces your critic's anger and hostility and gives you the opportunity to change, if you wish.

Setting Limits Many people (with the exception of two-year-olds) find 'no' the hardest word to say. If you need to refuse a request, try saying 'no' in two parts: the first part expresses your perception of the other person's position, the second part is your refusal to meet their request. This is often called an empathic 'no'. It softens the blow a little. For example:

Daughter: Can I borrow your car to go to the party?
Mother: (i) I understand that you want the car very badly,
            (ii) but I'm really not comfortable about lending it to
            you.

Negative Inquiry This skill is useful in situations in which you are unclear about what is being said, particularly when you are being criticized and you want to prompt the other person to give you more information (if relevant) or to exhaust the topic.

It helps the other person to be more direct and assertive with you and to clarify what is meant. Negative inquiry is an assertive, non-defensive, non-critical request for more specific information, to enable you to assess the value the criticism has for you. For example:

Manager: You didn't improve your performance this week.
Worker: I don't understand. What is it about my performance
          that you find unsatisfactory?

The message is: let us look at what I am doing that you don't like. Persist until you get all the information you need and find out what the criticism is really about.

With practice this skill allows you to be more comfortable in seeking out specific criticism about yourself, while prompting the other person to express negative opinions honestly and improve communication.

Fogging Fogging refers to the idea of creating a fog bank or screen as protection. It is referred to as 'agreeing in principle', 'agreeing with the odds', or 'agreeing with the half-truth'. It is a skill which can be useful for dealing with nagging or unwanted manipulative criticism. A fog bank offers no resistance, it does not fight back, is unaffected, persistent and opaque, and is very hard to deal with.

Fogging involves the acceptance of criticism by calmly acknowledging to your critic the probability that there may be *some* truth in what they have said. It allows you to be your own judge as to what you do. In fogging you do not deny the criticism, get defensive, give explanations, or counter-attack. You offer no resistance at all; instead you 'let your sail flap out of your critic's wind' so they lose the power to disturb you:

Mother: You were late home again.

Son: That's true, Mum, I was late.

Mother: If you stay out late you will get overtired and sick.

Son: You could be right, Mum, if I didn't stay out late so often I would get more sleep.

Mother: You need plenty of sleep if you are going to study successfully.

Son: I'm sure you're right, Mum, but I'm not worried about it.

Mother: You should be worried.

Son: You're probably right. When I start to feel concerned I'll do something about it.

This skill allows you to receive criticism reasonably comfortably and to take responsibility for your own actions, without becoming anxious or defensive and at the same time giving no reward to those using manipulative criticism. It is an irritating form of communication and should only be used when nagging continues after direct statements by you have been disregarded and you need to protect yourself from further attack.

Broken Record This skill is very useful in commercial situations, for example, in coping with door-to-door salesmen or when returning faulty goods. It enables you to persist in what you want without getting side-tracked.

It involves practising speaking as if you are stuck in the groove of a broken record. You calmly repeat what you want over and over again in a calm repetitive voice, until the person gives in or agrees to a compromise. You do not get angry, irritated or loud or allow yourself to be diverted into side issues, reasons or excuses. You must be persistent and refuse to be side-tracked. For example:

Shopper: I want to return this meat. I bought it yesterday and it is rotten now.

Salesman: There can't be anything wrong with it; no one else has complained.

Shopper: It is quite possible that no one else has complained, but this meat is rotten and I want to return it.

Salesman: You must have left the meat in the sun – our meat is not rotten.

Shopper: This meat is rotten and I want to return it.

This skill helps you avoid getting into arguments and helps you feel more comfortable in ignoring manipulative verbal side issues, baiting and irrelevant logic, while sticking to your desired point. It is a distancing form of communication which is likely to get you what you want but will not endear you to the other person.

These are some of the techniques you can practise when you start asserting yourself. Don't forget that for clear effective communication the verbal and the non-verbal messages need to be congruent.

The Five-Star Plan Here is a set of five points which I have found to be a useful guide in approaching situations assertively.

You can use it in various ways. Firstly, it is a very useful way of clarifying your own thoughts about a situation, particularly in separating facts from interpretations of, and feelings about, facts. The five points can then form the plan of an assertive statement, or the structure of a letter, each point becoming a paragraph. Use it as a guide only. Don't feel compelled to mention every point in every situation.

DESCRIBE   I describe the situation which bothers me, sticking closely to the facts and being concrete and specific: 'Last week you didn't show up for our meeting and I waited around for an hour.'

EXPRESS   I express my feelings about it in an 'I' statement: 'I felt angry with you for letting me down.'

UNDERSTAND   I indicate that I understand the other person's needs, feelings or situation if this is appropriate: 'I realize that you may have been very busy.'

SPECIFY   I specify clearly the actions which I want of the other person: 'Another time I would like you to let me know if you are unable to keep our appointment.'

OUTCOME   I mention the anticipated positive outcomes of change. I may also mention the negative aspects of no change: 'That way I can plan my time accordingly and I'll feel much better about you when we meet.'

When you have asserted yourself successfully, make sure you give yourself credit for the changes you are making.

How to Practise Assertiveness One of the best ways to practise assertiveness is through dramatizing a particular situation. In an assertion training course this is often done in groups of three.

If you are not in a course you might like to try it out with friends or, if you prefer, you could go through the steps yourself, either acting out the different roles alone or even writing it all down like a play.

If you have three people, one person (usually you) acts out your role, another can play the part of the person you want to be assertive with, and the third can be an observer. You can also reverse roles with your partner, to show how you would like to behave in a particular situation and how the other person might feel.

Because the observer is not involved in the action, they can watch you and give you important information about how you acted, whether your body language supported your words, whether you sounded as if you meant what you said, and so on. The observer can also make suggestions and help you think up appropriate words to use and ways of overcoming blocks. Reverse roles as suggested above, then go back to being you again and keep trying different approaches until you feel comfortable with your performance. Play acting allows you to learn by trial and error without the problems of a real life situation.

Here are some steps you can follow:
1 Describe the situation in detail.
2 Describe what you usually do to avoid asserting yourself – how you usually behave.
3 Explain why you would want to give that up and assert yourself instead. What do you want to accomplish?
4 What do you think might be stopping you from being assertive here?
   a Do you have some unrealistic beliefs about the consequences of being assertive? If so, what are they?
   b What do you see as your rights in this situation?
5 Are you anxious about asserting yourself? If so, how could you reduce your anxiety and feel more comfortable about being assertive?
6 Do you have all the information you need?
7 Prepare yourself now by role playing ways of handling your situation assertively.
8 Select whichever way feels reasonably comfortable and is most likely to achieve your goals in the real life situation.

After you have role-played how you would like to act and have practised it several times, try it out in real life. If possible, report back to your friends about the outcome. If it was not satisfactory, act out what happened and work on it again. Keep trying. Each time you succeed it gets easier and you become more comfortable and less anxious.

Use this list to evaluate your role play and your real life assertions. If your answers are 'no', keep role playing until you can answer 'yes'.

Did I say what I wanted to say?

Was I direct and unapologetic?

Did I stand up for my own rights without infringing the rights of the other person?

Was I sitting or standing in an assertive posture?

Did my voice sound strong and calm?

Were my gestures relaxed?

Did I feel good about myself after I finished speaking?

Am I satisifed with the way my assertion affected my relationships with the other people?

Remember that assertion and listening go hand in hand. When the relationship is important be prepared to switch back and forth between asserting yourself and listening with understanding to the other's response.

Appropriate Expression

Sometimes when people learn assertiveness they go in for assertion for the sake of assertion, or they go a bit overboard and become rather aggressive without realizing it. Similarly, when people hear about the value of self-disclosure they may get trapped in a 'tyranny of openness'. The aim of assertion training is to move away from 'oughts' and 'shoulds' and to gain access to a wider range of genuine choices.

Learning a new skill does not mean you have to use it all the time. Hopefully, your behavioural repertoire has broadened and you have more choices about the way you can act in a given situation. If you have learned to be comfortable about being assertive you can choose when and how it is appropriate for you to express yourself. When people know that they have the necessary skills to assert themselves, they frequently feel less of a need to do so. When they decide not to assert themselves, it is because they choose not to, not because they are afraid or unable to, and that makes all the difference in the world!

I hope that you have gained a greater sense of your freedom to choose and of your own personal power.

The Next Step

We have now come to the end of the journey through this book. Our trip has had a beginning, a middle and an end. It began with Self-Esteem, in the middle was Reflective Listening and it ended with Self-Assertion. You may, of course, have followed a different sequence.

You may have studied only one section of the book, perhaps as part of a course or training programme. If so I strongly recommend that you take some time now to read through the other sections. The discrete sections in this book are arbitrary separations – listening and assertion are two aspects of the one process. If you have developed one set of skills at the expense of the other it is only half the story. Furthermore, both sets of skills are inextricably connected with self-esteem, so it is important to read that section too.

Let us look back briefly over the territory covered in this book:

In part I on self-esteem, I explained the importance of a positive sense of self. Low self-esteem is like unnecessary baggage which weighs you down and leads you into a downward spiral or vicious circle. I suggested that even small changes in ways of thinking and feeling about yourself, and ways of behaving towards others, could be a turning point for positive new directions. Some suggestions for enhancing self-esteem were made including, in particular, learning better ways of communicating with others. The remaining sections of the book focused on two aspects of communication – listening to others and expressing oneself.

Part II on reflective listening was an opportunity to take time to reflect awhile about how other people are experiencing the world. We looked briefly at the process of communication and then at some of the consequences of different ways of responding to others. If you did the test called 'Your Response Style', you might like to do this test again now and compare the results. We explored in some detail three sets of skills required for listening and responding effectively: attending, following and reflecting.

In part III on self-assertion, I outlined some of the pitfalls associated with being non-assertive and how both submissive and aggressive behaviour connect with the downward spiral of low self-esteem and disrupted relationships. We explored some steps for approaching situations more assertively and some useful verbal skills, recognizing that along with personal rights goes personal responsibility.

Each person's world is different and each journey will be unique. This book will have guided some of you through familiar territory and may have been a reminder of inner resources and skills you had forgotten you had. Maybe it has also provided a new way of mapping your experience and helped to fill in some of the gaps.

For others, this book may have been a journey into the unknown. For you I hope this little guidebook will have proved useful in finding your way.

The purpose of a map or a guidebook is not to tell you where you should go but to provide you with some information and guidelines that you might need to help you orient yourself and find your direction.

Now that you have arrived at the end of this book, by whatever route, you may be wondering what your next steps might be.

Hopefully, you will by now have experienced the discovery of some strengths within yourself which maybe you were not aware of or had lost touch with. Hopefully too, you will have experienced the satisfaction and delight of those moments when you have tried something new and found it works.

Now is the time to consolidate what you have learned by

regularly practising the skills in this book. You will find that they need practice and more practice. It's easy to slip back into old habits. Don't worry if you slip back sometimes; it's the overall direction that counts.

Journeys are never smooth and even. There are rocky patches, boggy areas, some steep climbs, some stretches of desert, some brilliant sunrises and occasional oases. Life is like that; and change is like that too – two steps forward and one step back.

Don't be upset if sometimes you think of what you want to say after the event. This at least means that you are becoming more aware. You will find as you practise that the gap gets smaller and you get it right the first time more often than before. Sometimes it is even possible to correct yourself on the spot and admit your slip, for example, you might say, 'Let's start again, what I meant to say was . . .' Where goodwill exists your efforts to communicate clearly and honestly will usually be appreciated.

You may find when you are trying out new skills that you feel a bit anxious. Don't let this put you off either. Anxiety can be a sign that you are breaking new ground, and therefore it can be seen as a sign of progress. Take it easy and rest awhile in between each new venture. Don't push yourself too hard but keep practising. People who pioneer new territory need time and space to rest, build up their energy and consolidate their new achievements.

Books and courses which deal with personal and emotional issues sometimes touch on particularly sensitive areas for some people and open up barely healed wounds. If reading this book has left you feeling undermined in any way or unduly upset, recognize this as an opportunity to resolve this issue and let it go. Seek out an understanding friend or a professional counsellor to assist you to sort it out, so that you can get on with your life.

Those of you who want to extend and develop the ideas and skills explored in this book, at a deeper level, might like to take up one or more of the following options:

1 Set yourself goals and practise regularly. If you find you are slipping back, get the book out again and remind yourself of where you want to go.

2 Look up some of the suggestions for further study at the end of this book.

3 Follow up some of the other references listed as source material at the end of the book.
4 Join a group where you can extend your experience and practise some of the skills you feel are most important for you.

I hope you have found this book to be a worthwhile and enjoyable experience. You will find you can adapt these skills to many more situations than those already mentioned.

We live in a challenging world of cultural and ideological diversity, rapid technological change, inequality, exploitation, oppression and violence on a personal, community and global scale, and overall – the threat of annihilation.

To even begin to address these issues, let alone survive them, we need people with as much self-esteem, inner wisdom and creativity as they can muster – people who can find a balance between listening with respect and understanding and appropriately taking a stand and asserting themselves.

149

Building up your own sense of self-worth and improving your own communication skills can assist you in becoming just such a person.

Suggestions for Further Study

I Self-Esteem

Books

Michele & Craig Borba, *Self-Esteem: A Classroom Affair*, Harper & Row, San Francisco, 1978.
This book includes 101 ways to help children like themselves – and more. It has heaps of tried and true practical activities and games for making children happy and for creating an environment in which they can learn to like themselves. A great book for teachers, parents and anyone else who cares for children. A book about self-enhancement.

Benjamin Hoff, *The Tao of Pooh*, Methuen, UK, 1982.
'In which is revealed,' according to the subtitle, 'that one of the world's greatest Taoist masters isn't Chinese ... but is in fact A. A. Milne's bear of little brain – Winnie-the-Pooh.' A delightful little book. Read it to enjoy the illustrations and to appreciate your own inner simplicity and wisdom.

Matthew McKay & Patrick Fleming, *Self-Esteem: A Proven Program of Cognitive Technique for Assessing, Improving and Maintaining Your Self-Esteem*, New Harbinger Publishers, Oakland, USA, 1987.
Don't be put off by the somewhat alarming sub-title. This book has excellent chapters on: handling mistakes, criticism, hypnosis,

assertion and shoulds. An excellent book to read when you have finished this one.

Audio Tapes

Nathaniel Branden, *How to Build Self-Esteem*, Psychology Today Cassettes, Ziff Davis Publication Co., NY, 1980.
This tape is a must. If you are not too put-off by the very American style of the interviewer, you will want to listen to it over and over again. I'm sure it will touch some personal chords.

II Listening

Books

Robert Bolton, *People Skills*, Prentice-Hall, Englewood Cliffs, NJ, 1979.
If you want to expand on the points I have made, I suggest you read this book next. I like it so much I've drawn on it heavily. As well as the chapters on reflective listening it also contains excellent material on assertion and conflict management skills.

Gerard Egan, *You and Me: The Skills of Communicating and Relating to Others*, Brooks Cole, Monterey, California, 1977.
Contains a systematic step-by-step approach to becoming more self-aware, developing interpersonal skills and learning to become more active and outgoing in relating to others. It's full of useful activities and exercises you can do to practise.

David Johnson, *Reaching Out: Interpersonal Effectiveness and Self-Actualization*, Prentice-Hall, Englewood Cliffs, New Jersey, 1981.
Focuses on the interpersonal skills needed for reaching out to others to build and maintain friendships; good mixture of theory and practice; written in a non-technical style; delightful cartoons. There are sections on self-disclosure, expressing feelings, listening and responding, genuineness and respect, effective group participation and plenty of useful exercises.

Virginia Satir, *Peoplemaking*, Science and Behavioral Books, Palo Alto, California, 1972.
This is one of those books that people frequently borrow and like so much they forget to return. It has great cartoons, is lively and easy to read, and is very sound and informative. You're sure to recognize all your friends in it and your own family – maybe even yourself! As a leading family therapist, Virginia Satir takes a systems approach to people. Topics include: self-esteem, how we affect one another in the family or other systems in which we live, the characteristics of nurturing systems and destructive systems, defensive vs levelling styles of communication, family rules – in short how people are made. I thoroughly recommend this book to anyone interested in people, particularly to parents, teachers and caregivers.

III Self-Assertion

Books

Robert Bolton, *People Skills*, Prentice-Hall, Englewood Cliffs, NJ, 1979.

Sharon & Gordon Bower, *Asserting Yourself: A Practical Guide for Positive Change*, Addison Wesley, Reading, Massachusetts, 1976.
A very detailed and useful account of the DESC Script on which I based my 5-star plan, with many examples of how it can be applied and words to use.

Diane Bretherton *et al.*, *Dealing with Conflict*, MCAE, Melbourne, 1987.
A practical course for secondary students and young adults containing activities and handouts. Sections on assessing and binding a group, dealing with conflict, and extra practice in communications. Successfully trialed in schools.

Pamela Butler, *Self-Assertion for Women: A Guide to Becoming Androgynous*, Harper & Row, New York, 1976.
This book is written by a woman for women, yet I find myself

constantly recommending it to men too, because it's good and they need it. Particularly useful chapter on dealing with criticism.

Marjorie Manthei, *Positively Me*, Reed Methuen, Auckland, 1981.
A very readable and practical guidebook for people working on assertion skills either alone or informally in groups; or for group leaders without the time to organise a programme. Throughout the book are STOP points, where important issues for discussion are raised. Written by a very experienced group leader in New Zealand.

Audio Tapes

Julio J. Guerra, Sherwin B. Cotter & Susan Morgan Cotler, *A Guide to Self-Dignity*, Assertion Training Series, Research Press, Champaign, Illinois, 1976.
A set of four tapes dealing with various aspects of assertion. Particularly good on demonstrating conversation skills – starting, maintaining and ending conversations – and on demonstrating ways of standing up for yourself when under attack.

Source Material

Alberti, R. E. & Emmons, M. L., *Your Perfect Right: A Guide to Assertive Behavior*, Impact, San Louis, California, 1974.

Back, K., *Assertiveness at Work: A Practical Guide to Handling Awkward Situations*, McGraw Hill, UK, 1982.

Bloom, L. Z., Coburn, K. & Pearlman, J., *The New Assertive Woman*, Delaconte Press, NY, 1975.

Bolton, R., *People Skills*, Prentice-Hall, Englewood Cliffs, NJ, 1979.

Borba, M. & C., *Self-Esteem: A Classroom Affair: 101 Ways to Help Children Like Themselves . . . and more*, Harper & Row, San Francisco, 1978.

Bower, S. A. & Bower, G. H., *Asserting Yourself: A practical guide for positive change*, Addison Wesley, 1976.

Bradshaw, P., *Personal Power: How to Build Self-Esteem and Improve Performance*, Prentice-Hall, Englewood Cliffs, NJ, 1983.

Brammer, L. M., *The Helping Relationship: Process and Skills*, Prentice-Hall, Englewood Cliffs, NJ, 1979.

Branden, N., *The Psychology of Self-Esteem: A New Concept of Man's Psychological Nature*, Bantam, NY, 1971.

Bretherton, D., *Active Listening*, (unpublished), IECD, Melbourne, 1981.

Bretherton, D., *Dealing with Conflict*, MCAE, Melbourne, 1987.

Burley-Allen, M., *Listening: The Forgotten Skill*, John Wiley, NY, 1982.

Butler, P., *Self-Assertion: A guide to becoming androgynous*, Harper & Row, New York, 1976.

Carkhuff, R. R. *et al.*, *The Art of Helping* (3rd edn), Human Resource Development Press, Amherst, Massachusetts, 1977.

Combs, A., Avila, D. I. & Purkey, W. W., *Helping Relationships: Basic Concepts for the Helping Professions*, Allyn & Bacon, Boston, 1975.

Combs, A., Blune, A., Newman, A. & Wass, H. L., *The Professional Education of Teachers: A Humanistic Approach to Teacher Preparation*, Ch. 5, Allyn & Bacon, Boston, 1975.

Cotler, S. B. & Guerra, J. J., *Assertion Training: A Humanistic Behavioral Guide to Self-Dignity*, Research Press, Champaign, Illinois, 1976.

Dinkmeyer, D. & McKay, G. D., *Systematic Training for Effective Parenting: Parents' Handbook*, American Guidance Service, Circles Pines, Minnesota, 1976.

Egan, G., *Interpersonal Living: A Skills/Contract Approach to Human-Relations Training in Groups*, Brooks/Cole, Monterey, California, 1976.

Egan, G., *The Skilled Helper: A Model for Systematic Helping and Interpersonal Relating*, Brooks/Cole, Monterey, California, 1975.

Egan, G., *Exercises in Helping Skills: A Training Manual to Accompany the Skilled Helper*, Brooks/Cole, Monterey, California, 1975.

Egan, G., *You and Me: The Skills of Communicating and Relating to Others*, Brooks Cole, Monterey, California, 1977.

Ellis, A. & Harper, R. A., *A New Guide to Rational Living*, Wilshire, California, 1977.

Ernst, F. Jnr., *Who's Listening? A Handbook of the Transactional Analysis of the Listening Function*, Addresso'set, Vallejo, California, 1973.

Fensterheim, H. & Baer, J., *Don't Say Yes When You Want to Say No*, New Dell Ed, NY, 1976.

Fisher, R. & Urey, W., *Getting to Yes*, Hutchinson, 1981.

Frederick, J., Unpublished papers, University of Melbourne Counselling Service, 1978.

Frey, D. C., *Enhancing Self-Esteem*, Accelerated Development Inc., Muncie, Indiana, 1984.

Fromm, E., *Man for Himself*, A Fawcett Premier Book, Holt Rinehart & Winston, New York, 1947.

Gazda, G., *Human Relations Development: A Manual for Education*, Allyn & Bacon, Boston, 1973.

Gordon, T., *P.E.T. Parent Effectiveness Training: The Tested New Way to Raise Responsible Children*, Peter Wyden, NY, 1970.

Hoff, B., *The Tao of Pooh*, Methuen, UK, 1982.

Howe, M., *Developing Helping Skills*, Swinburne Institute of Technology, Applied Behavioural Studies Centre, Hawthorn, Victoria, 1978.

Jakubowski, P. & Lange, A. J., *The Assertive Option, Your Rights and Responsibilities*, Ch. 7, Research Press, Champaign, Illinois, 1978.

Johnson, D. W., *Human Relations and Your Career: A Guide to Interpersonal Skills*, Prentice Hall, NJ, 1978.

Johnson, D. W., *Reaching Out: Interpersonal Effectiveness and Self-Actualization* (2nd edn), Chs. 4 & 7, Prentice-Hall, Englewood Cliffs, New Jersey, 1981.

Jourard, S. M., *The Transparent Self*, Van Nostrand, NY, 1971.

Lange, A. J. & Jakubowski, P., *Responsible Assertive Behaviour: Cognitive/Behavioral Procedures for Trainers*, Research Press, Champaign, Illinois, 1976.

Madders, Jane, *Stress and Relaxation: Self help ways to cope with stress and relieve nervous tension, ulcers, insomnia, migraine and high blood pressure*, Collins, Sydney, 1979.

Manthei, M., *Positively Me* (revised edn), Reed Methuen, Auckland, 1981.

McKay, M. PhD & Fleming, P., *Self-Esteem: A Proven Program of Cognitive Techniques for Assessing, Improving and Maintaining Your Self-Esteem*, New Harbinger Publishers, Oakland, California, 1987.

Mayeroff, M., *On Caring*, Harper & Row, NY, 1971.

Montgomery, B. & Evans, L., *You and Stress: A guide to successful living*, Nelson, Melbourne, 1984.

Moustakas, C. E., *Who Will Listen? Children and Parents in Therapy*, Ballantyne, NY, 1975.

Natalicio, L. & Hereford, C., *The Teacher as a Person*, Chs. 4 & 8, William Brown & Co., Dubuque, Iowa, 1972.

Phelps, S. & Austin, N., *The Assertive Woman*, Impact, St Louis, California, 1975.

Purkey, A. & William, W., *Self-Concept and School Achievement*, Prentice-Hall, Englewood Cliffs, NJ, 1970.

Powell, J., *The Secret of Staying in Love*, Argus Communications, Niles, Illinois, 1974.

Rogers, C. R., *Client-Centred Therapy*, Houghton Mifflin, Boston, 1951.

Rogers, C. R., 'My Philosophy of Interpersonal Relations and How it Grew', *Journal of Humanistic Psychology*, No. 13, 2, 1973.

Rogers, C., *On Personal Power: Inner strength and its revolutionary impact*, Delacorte Press, NY, 1977.

Rogers, C. R., 'The Necessary and Sufficient Conditions of Therapeutic Personality Change', *Journal of Consultative Psychology*, No. 21, 1957.

Satir, V., *Making Contact*, Celestial Arts, Millbrae, California, 1976.

Satir, V., *Peoplemaking*, Science and Behavior Books, Palo Alto, California, 1972.

Satir, V., *Self-Esteem*, Celestial Arts, Millbrae, California, 1975.

Seabury, D., *The Art of Selfishness*, Simon & Schuster, NY, 1964.

Schlen, A. & Ashcroft, N., *Human Territories: How We Behave in Space-Time*, Prentice-Hall, Englewood Cliffs, NJ, 1976.

Smith, M. J., *When I Say No, I Feel Guilty*, Dial Press, NY, 1975.

Taubman, B., *How to Become an Assertive Woman: The Key to Self-Fulfillment*, Pocket Books, NY, 1976.

Zastow, C., *Talk to Yourself Using the Powers of Self-Talk*, Prentice-Hall, Englewood Cliffs, NJ, 1979.

Audio Tapes

Alberti, R. & Emmons, M., *Assertiveness Training*, Psychology Today Cassettes, PO Box 278, Pratt Station, Brooklyn, NY 11205, USA.

Branden, N., *Building Self-Esteem*, Psychology Today Cassettes, PO Box 278, Pratt Station, Brooklyn, NY 11205, USA.

Guerra, J. J., Cotler, S. B. & Cotler, S. M., *A Guide to Self Dignity*, 1976. (4 tapes) Assertion Training Series Research Press, 2612 North Mattis Ave., Champaign, Illinois 61820, USA.

Viscott, D., *How to Listen to Your Feelings*, Psychology Today Cassettes, PO Box 278, Pratt Station, Brooklyn, NY 11205, USA.